The Illuminated Torah

By Sherri Jacobs, MS, LMFT, MA, ATR

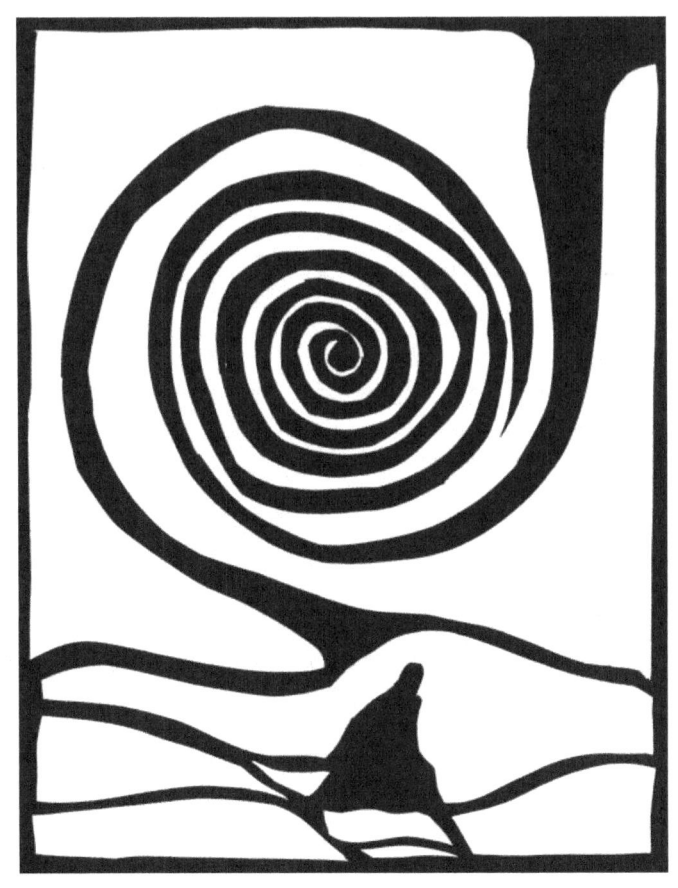

Dear Reader and fellow artist,

The images in this book are copies of a series of hand cut paper cuts created by artist and art therapist, Sherri Jacobs. Each image correlates to one of 54 sections of the Hebrew Bible.

This book is designed as a coloring book for adults and children. Is coloring really therapeutic? The rhythmic pattern of enhancing an image with color can be a soothing and mindful activity. The recent proliferation of the adult coloring book market is perhaps a response to a society living with extreme levels of stress and anxiety.

Many of the adult coloring books tend to have very complex patterns, causing undue frustration for older eyes, or individuals with less than stellar motor skills. The paper cut images in this book were designed with much broader spaces for coloring, with the hopes that it truly can be a soothing activity for people of all ages.

For questions, feedback, ideas, or more information, please contact Sherri Jacobs at:
heartlandarttherapy@gmail.com

Quote and references sourced from: Scherman, N. (1999) *The Chumash: Stone Edition of the Art Scroll Chumash Edition 1*. New York: Mesorah Publications, Ltd.

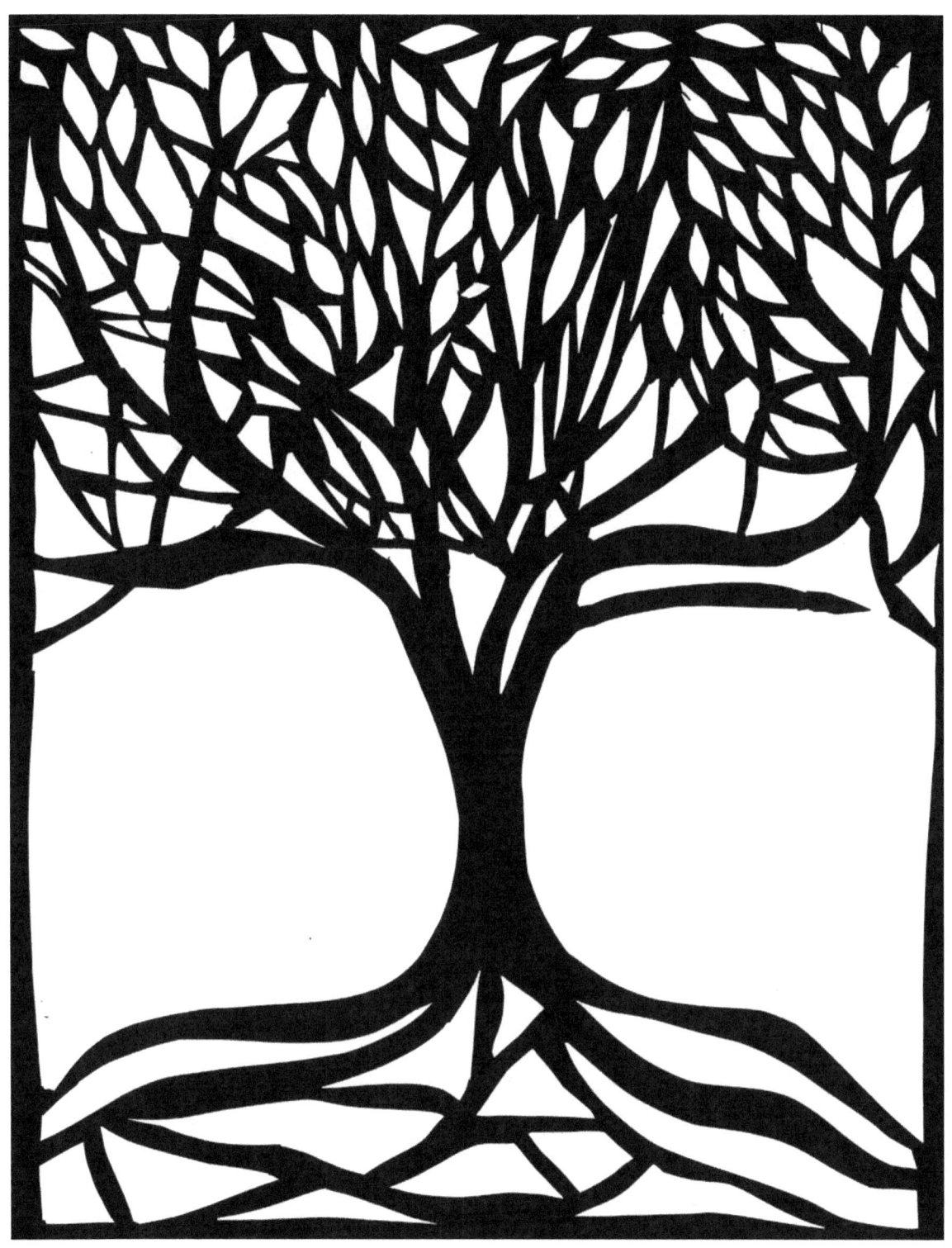

Bereishit *Genesis 1:1–6:8*

The creation story is followed by the first rebellious act of eating from the forbidden tree of knowledge of good and evil. This tree represents the expulsion of humans from the Garden of Eden.

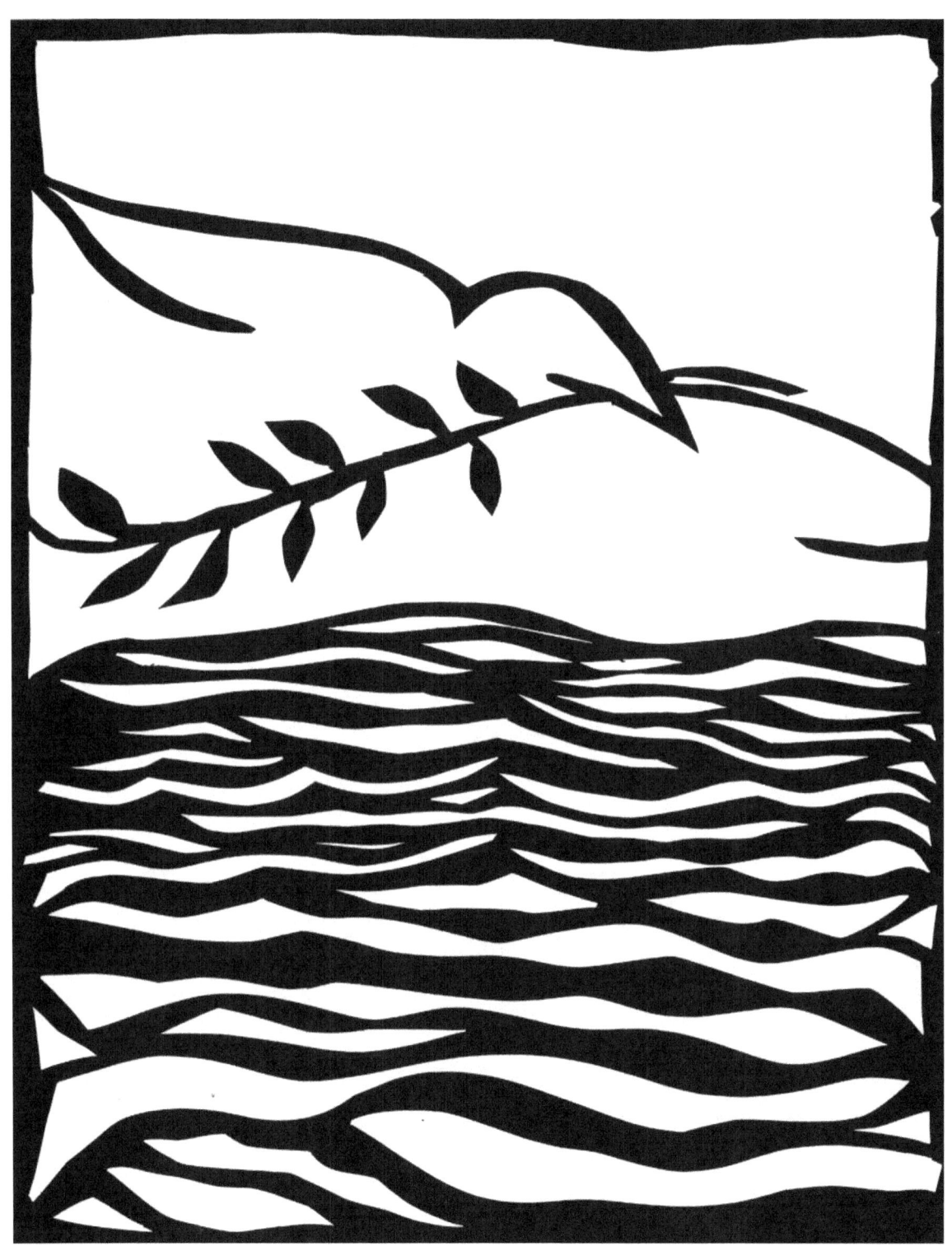

Noach *Genesis 6:9-11:32*

Following a flood lasting for forty days and forty nights, Noah sends a raven out from his ark in search of dry land. The raven does not return, and later a dove is sent out. The dove returns with an olive branch, signifying the end of the their tumultuous journey.

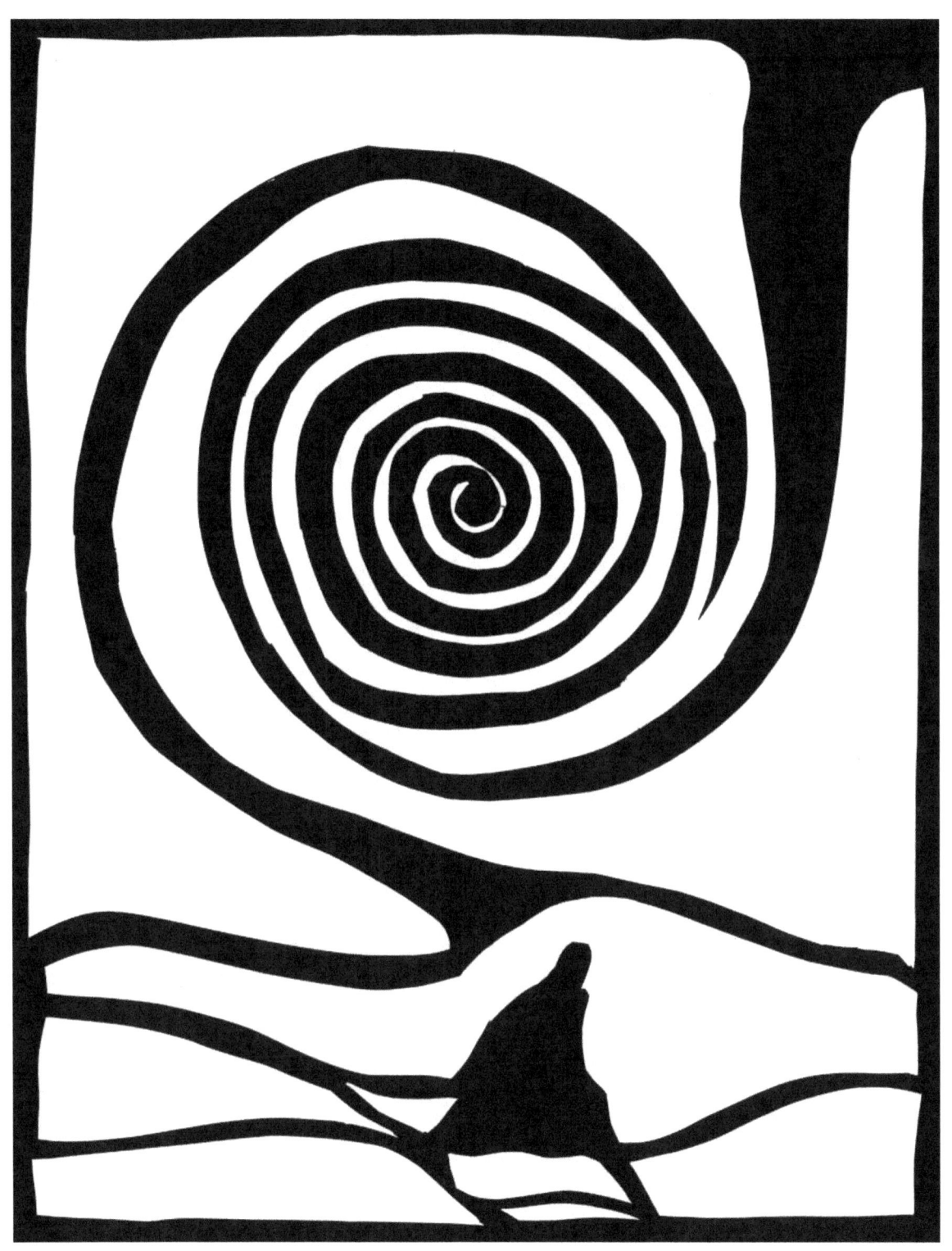

Lech Lecha   *Genesis 12:1–17:27*

Abraham, a man surrounded by idolatry, contemplates a different reality, and discovers the path of Monotheism. He is instructed to leave his land, his home, and his family to journey to a distant place, and fulfill his destiny.

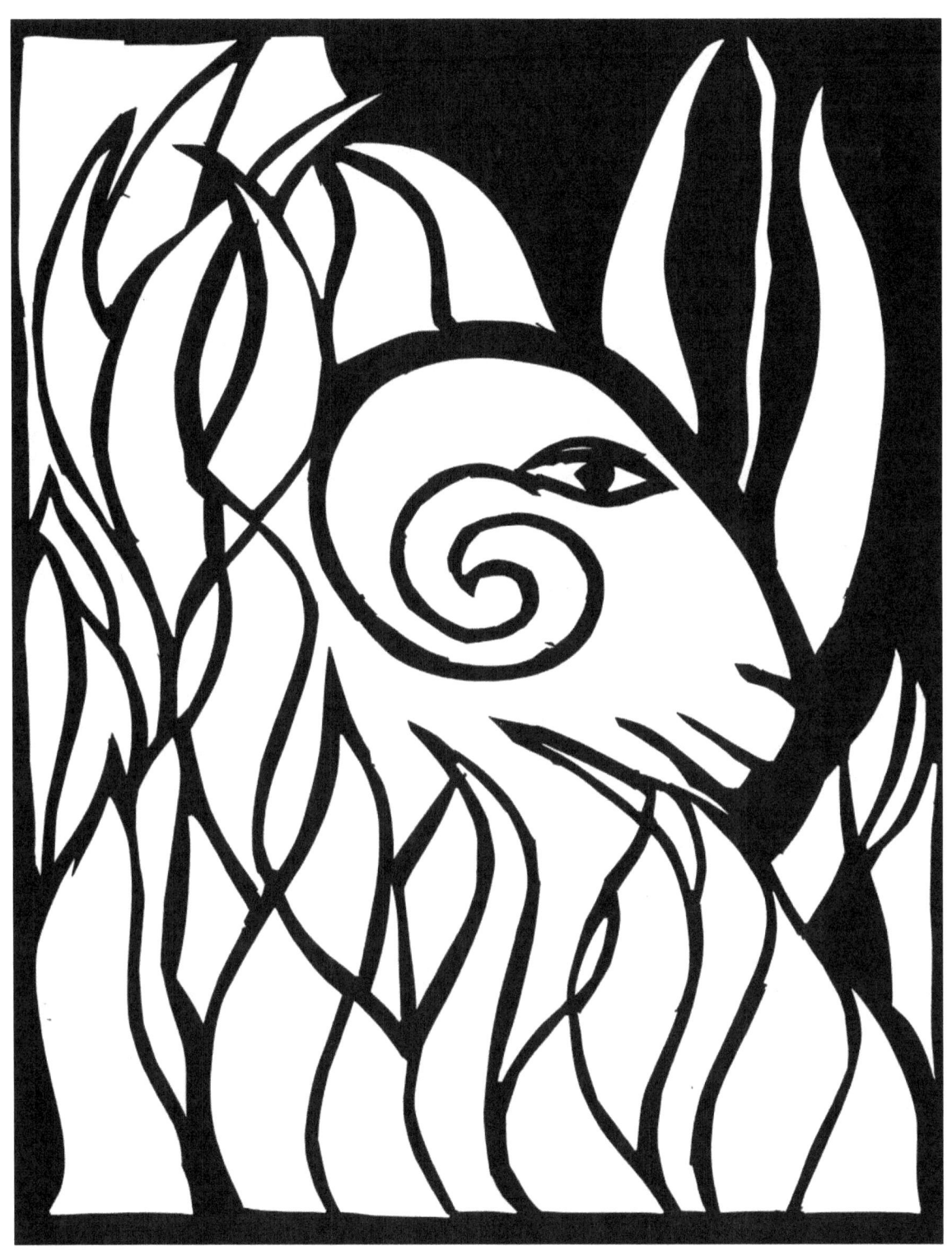

Vayeira *Genesis 18:1–22:24*

Abraham is tasked with sacrificing his only son, Isaac, as a test of his trust in God. At the last moment, a ram appears in the thicket to be sacrificed in place of Abraham's beloved son.

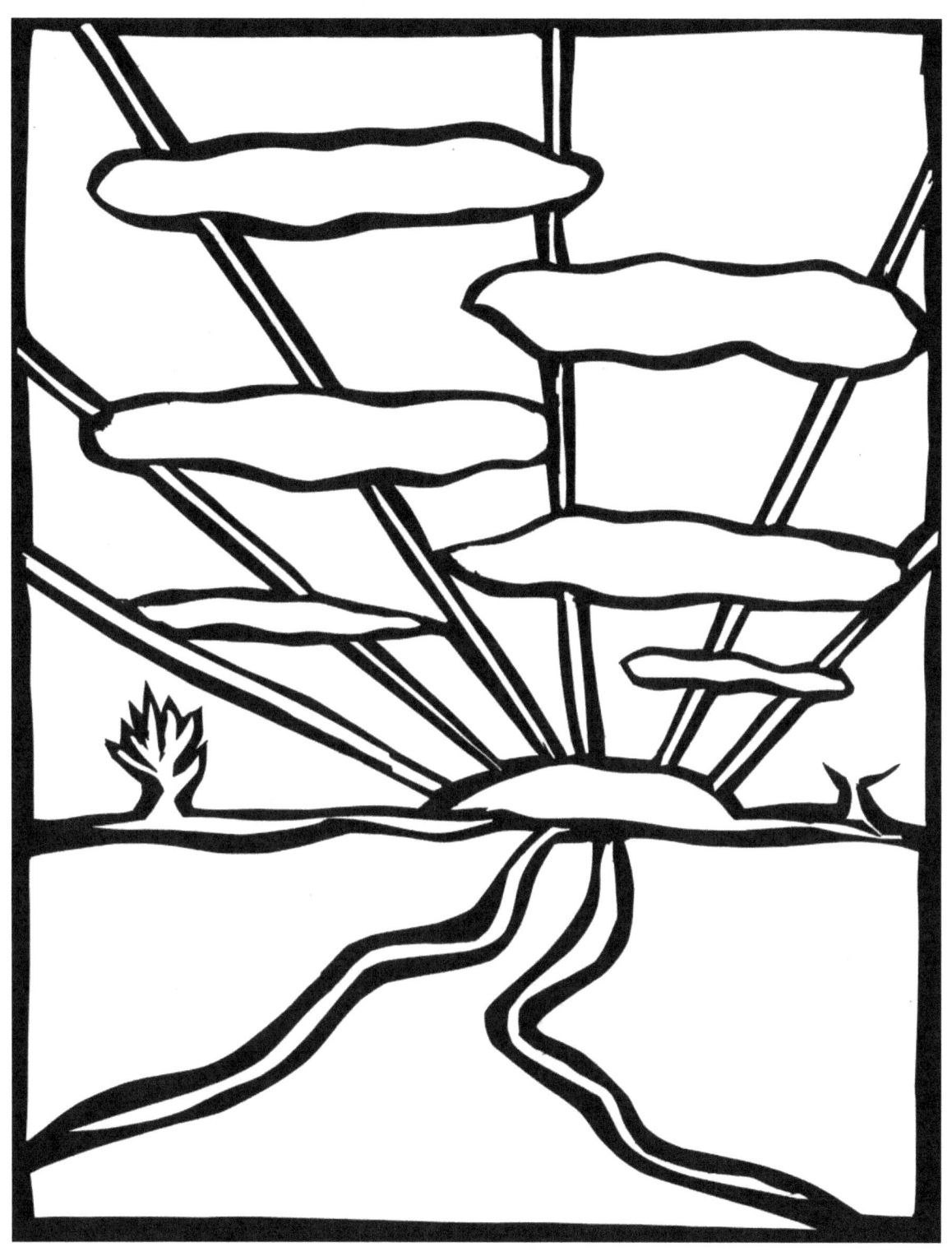

Chayei Sarah *Genesis 23:1-25:18*

This story explores the death of Sarah, Abraham's beloved wife. While Sarah was alive, the Oral Tradition states that clouds of glory hovered over the community. The departing clouds in this image commemorate her death.

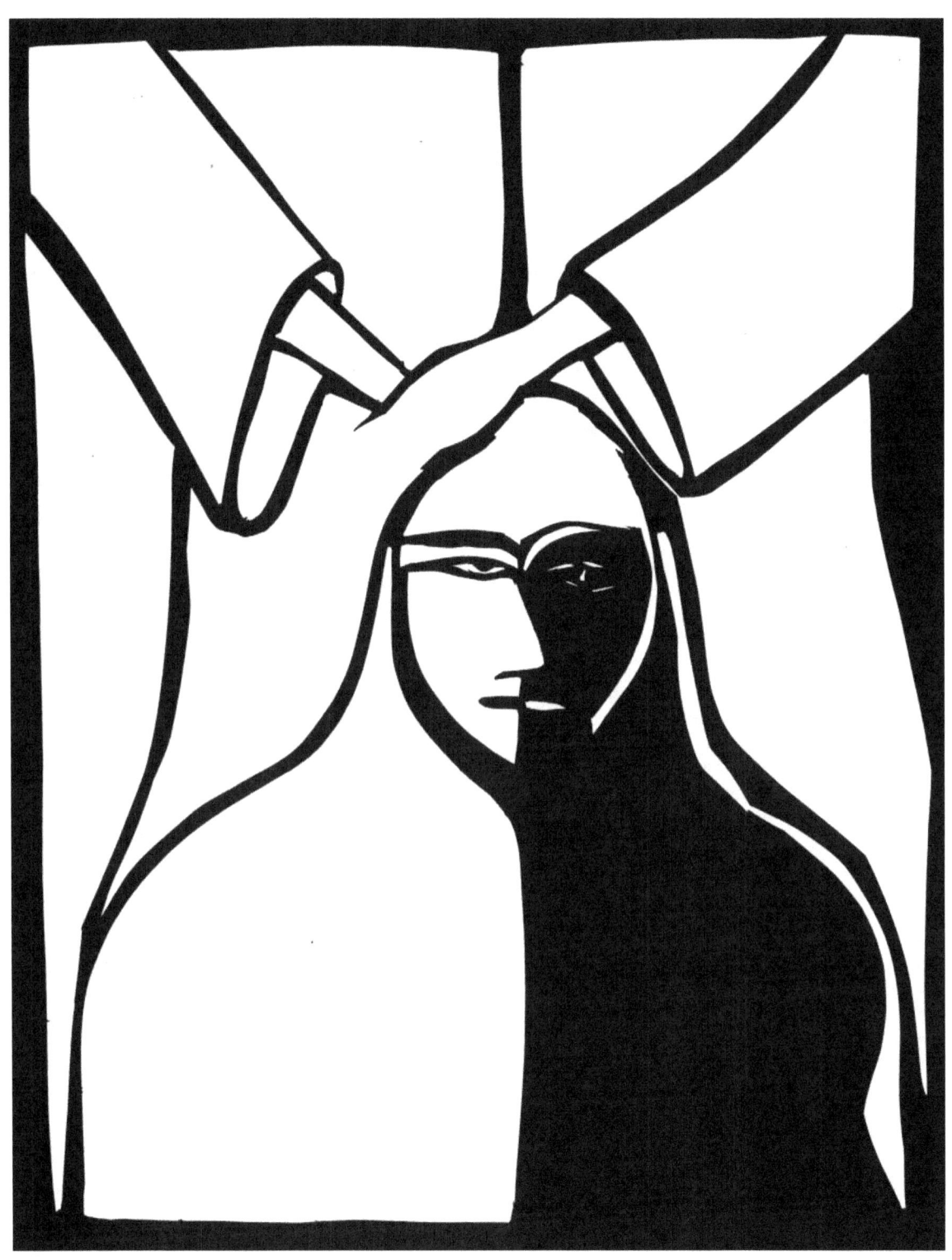

Toldot *Genesis 25:19-28:9*

Jacob, the son of Isaac, receives his father's blessing while posing as his twin, Esau. Although Jacob secures the blessing from his twin by trading it for a bowl of soup, his deceit leads to severe the internal conflict.

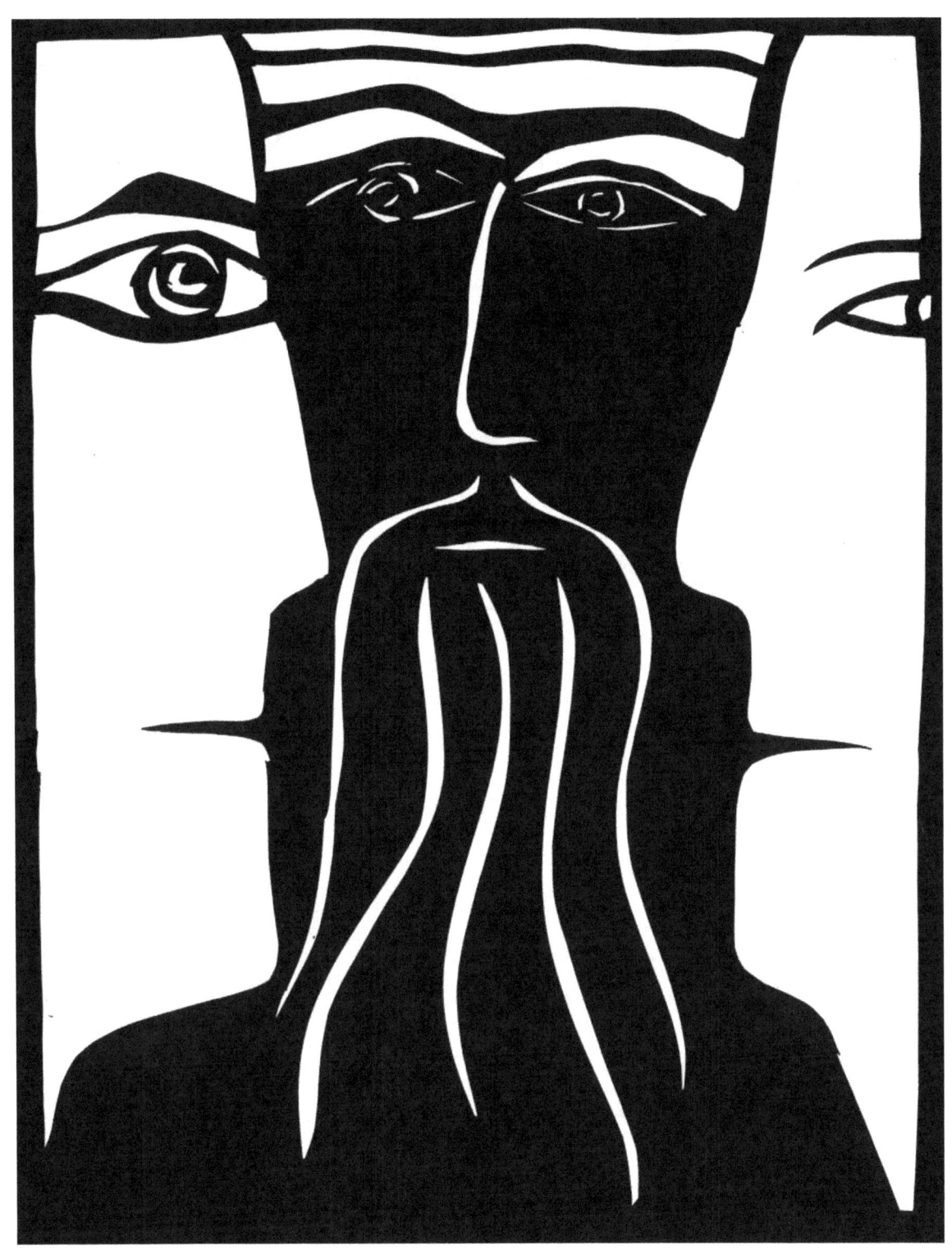

Vayeitzei *Genesis 28:10-32:3*

Jacob works for seven years to earn the right to marry Rachel, but is deceived into marrying Leah, whose identity is hidden under her wedding veil. Jacob is forced to work another seven years until he is granted the privilege of marrying Rachel.

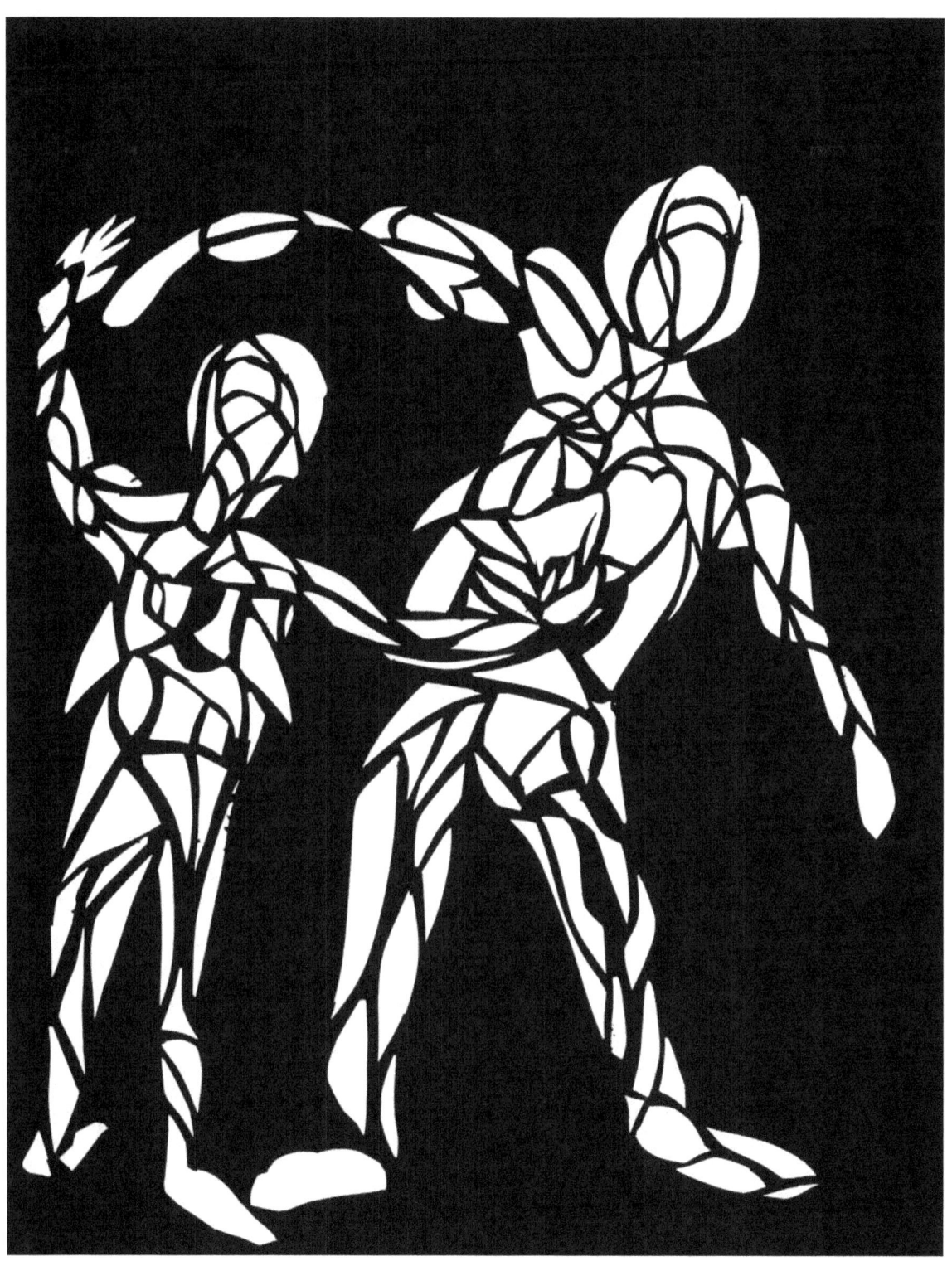

Vayishlach *Genesis 32:4-36:43*

In this story, Jacob prepares for an encounter with his estranged brother Esau. This story also recounts Jacob's wrestling match with a celestial being. This image depicts both experiences.

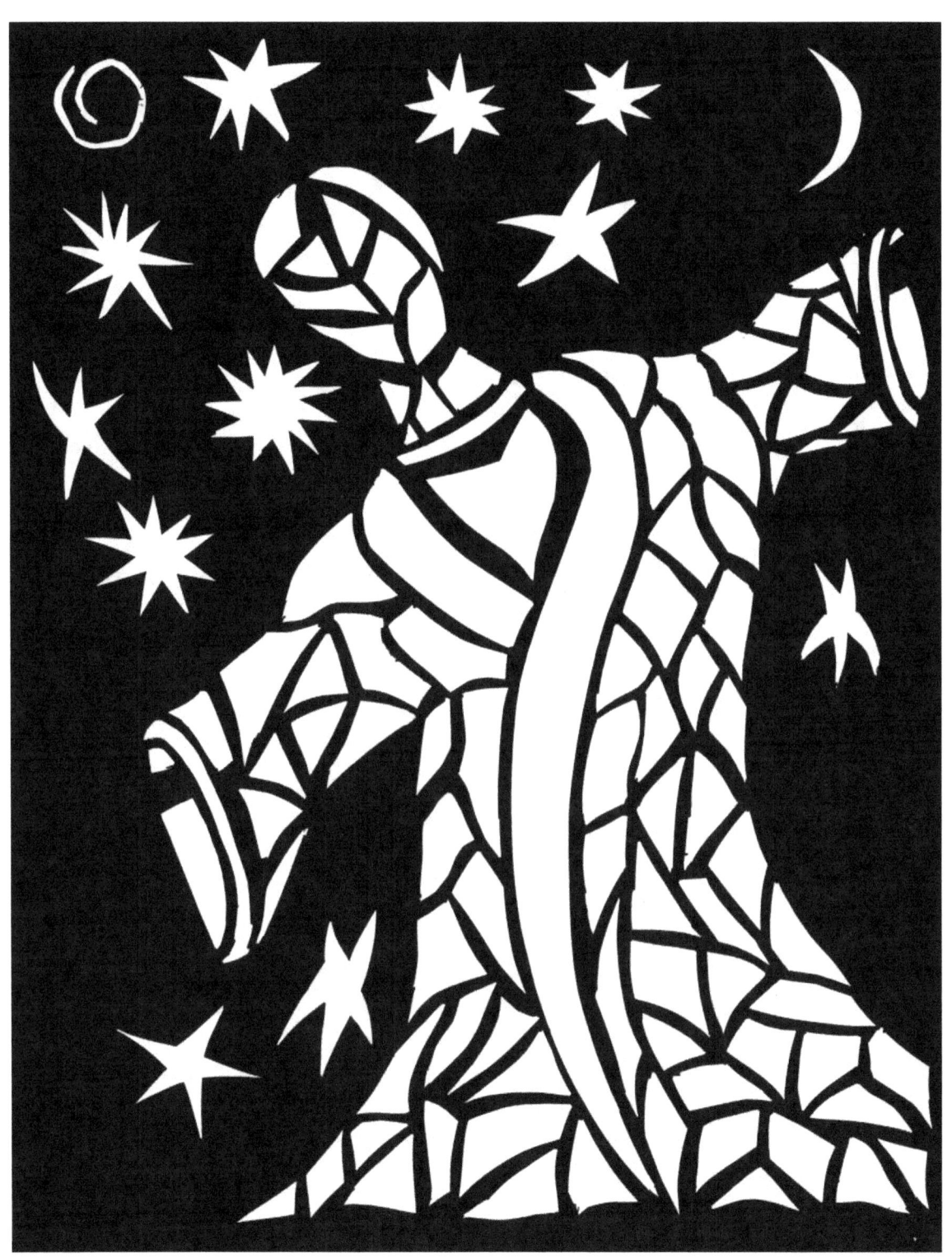

Vayeishev *Genesis 37:1–40:23*

Joseph, the favorite of Jacob's twelve sons, is given a beautiful coat. Out of jealousy, his brothers throw Joseph into a pit to die, but then decide sell him to people in a passing caravan.

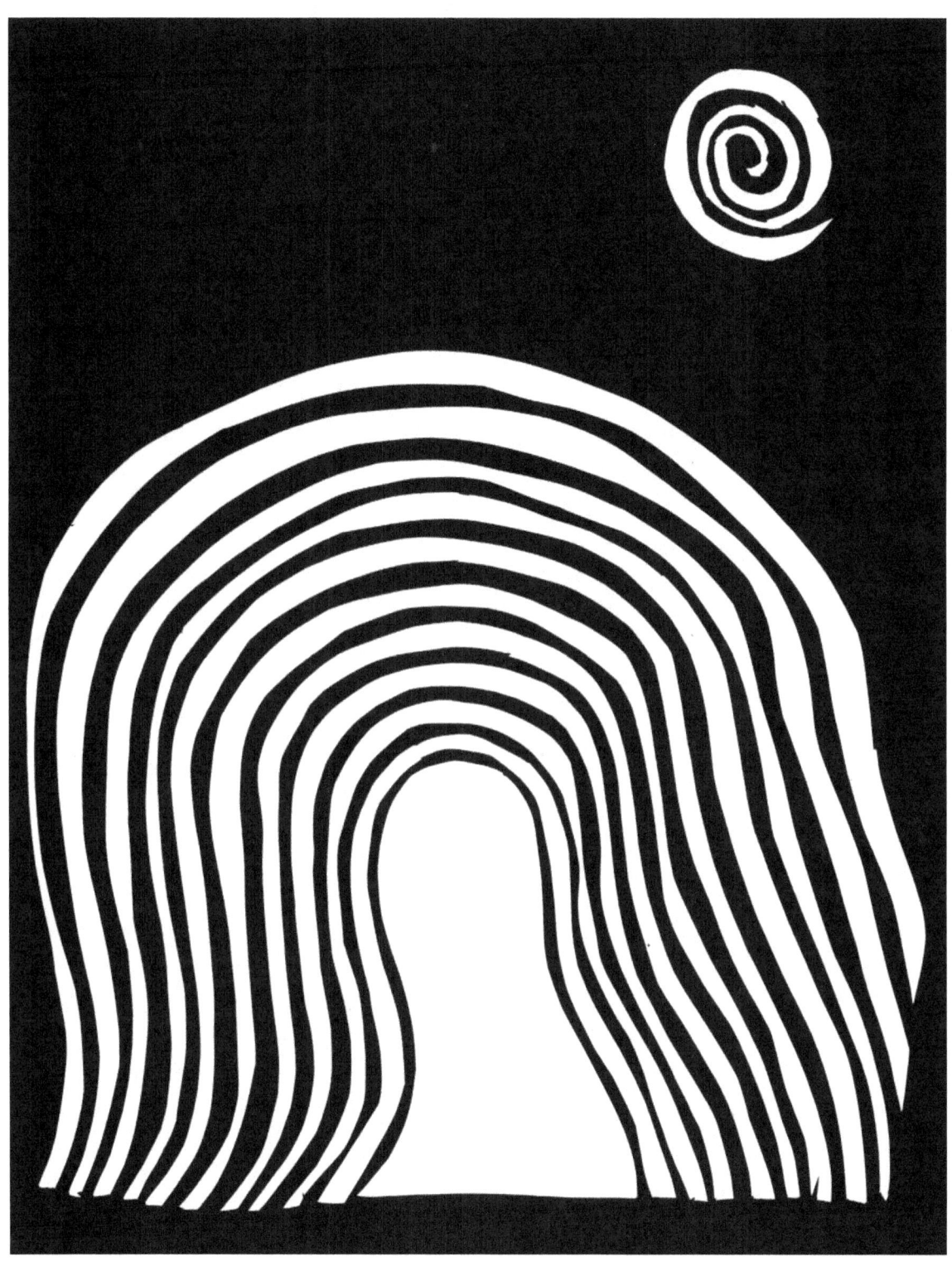

Mikeitz *Genesis 41:1-44:17*

The brothers journey to Egypt during a famine, and encounter their estranged brother Joseph, who is now an Egyptian leader. The brothers' concern for their youngest brother Benjamin is tested by Joseph, before he reveals his identity to them.

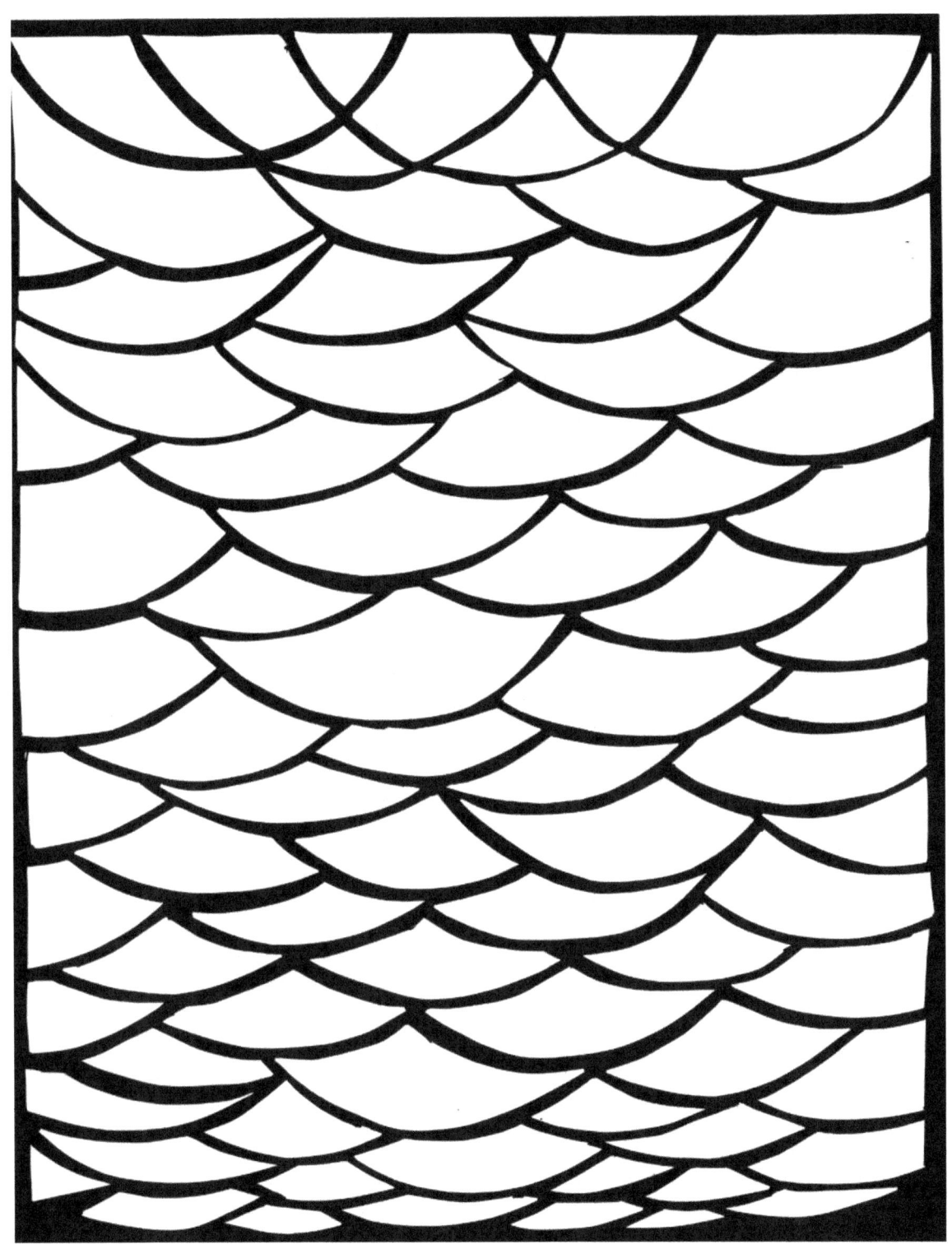

Vayigash *Genesis 44:18-47:27*

After learning of Joseph's identity and role in Egypt, Jacob's family (seventy souls in all) is invited to live in Egypt for food, protection, and a new life. The symbolism is depicted here through seventy half circles.

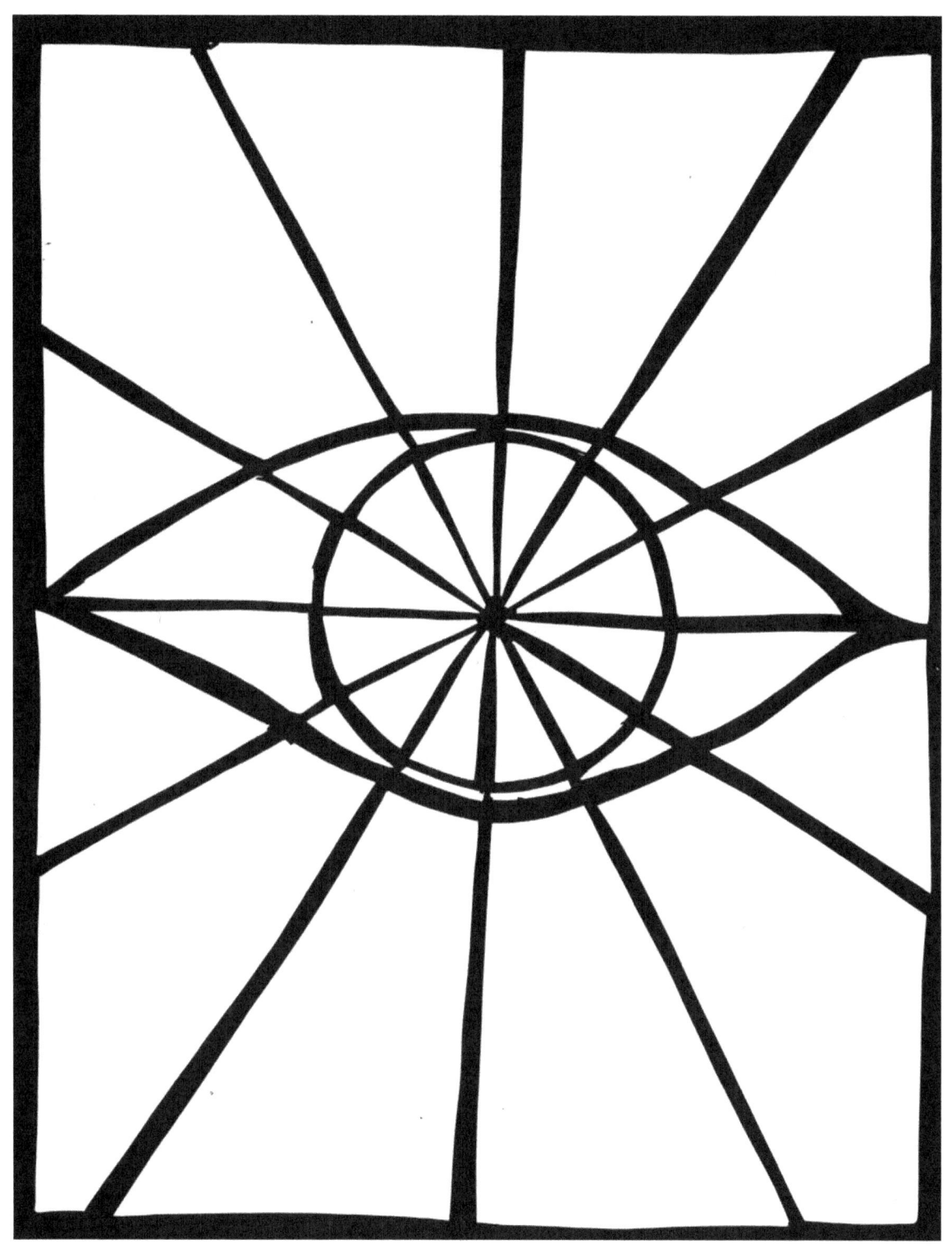

Vayechi *Genesis 47:28-50:26*

At the end of his life, Jacob blesses each of his twelve children. The imagery of an eye wide open hints at Jacob's previous experience of deceiving his father Isaac, who was blind.

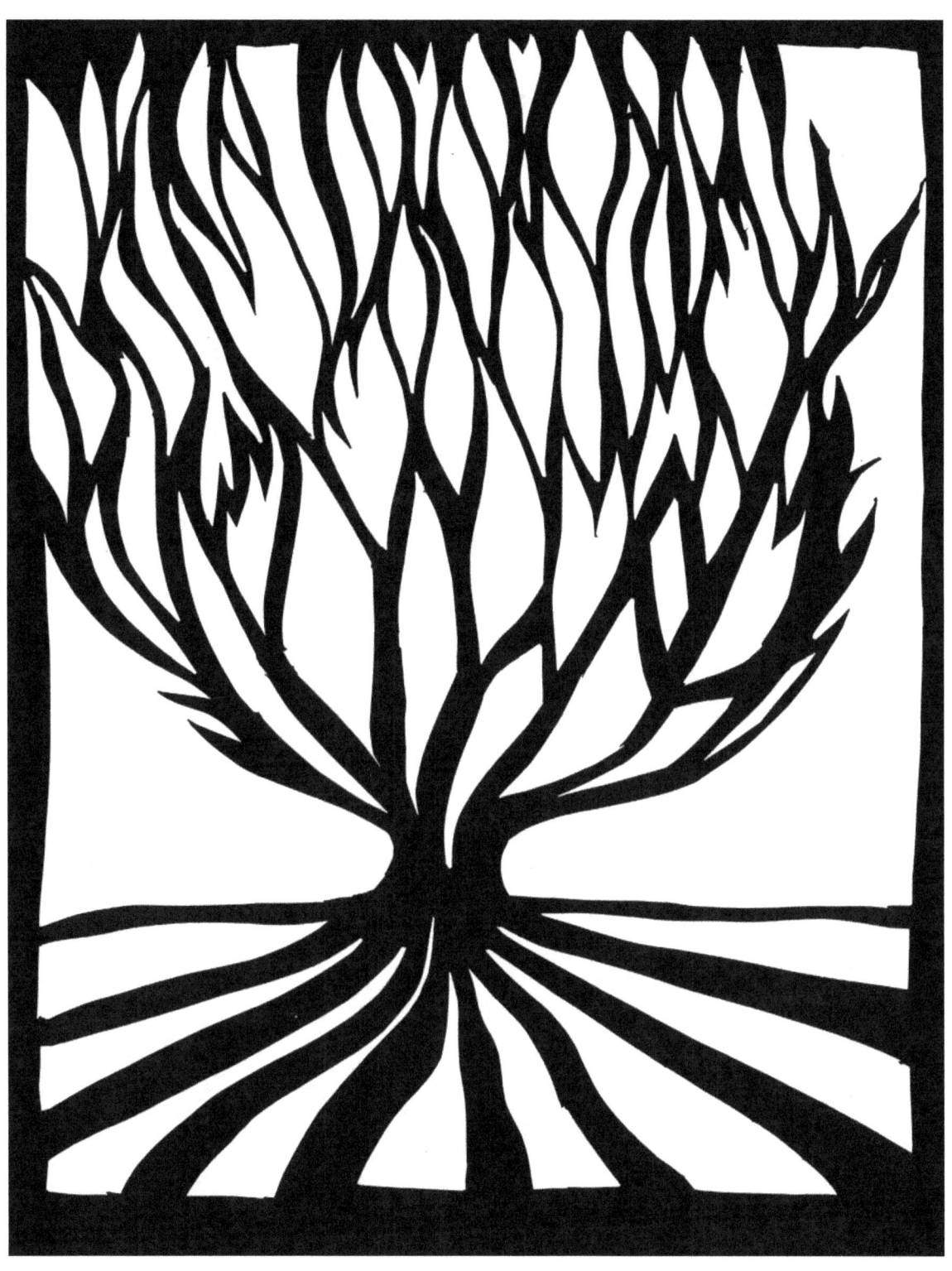

Shemot *Exodus 1:1 - 6*

In this story, we are introduced to Moses. Through his unusual encounter with a burning bush that was not consumed by fire, Moses learns of his future role as the leader of his people, and role in emancipating them from slavery.

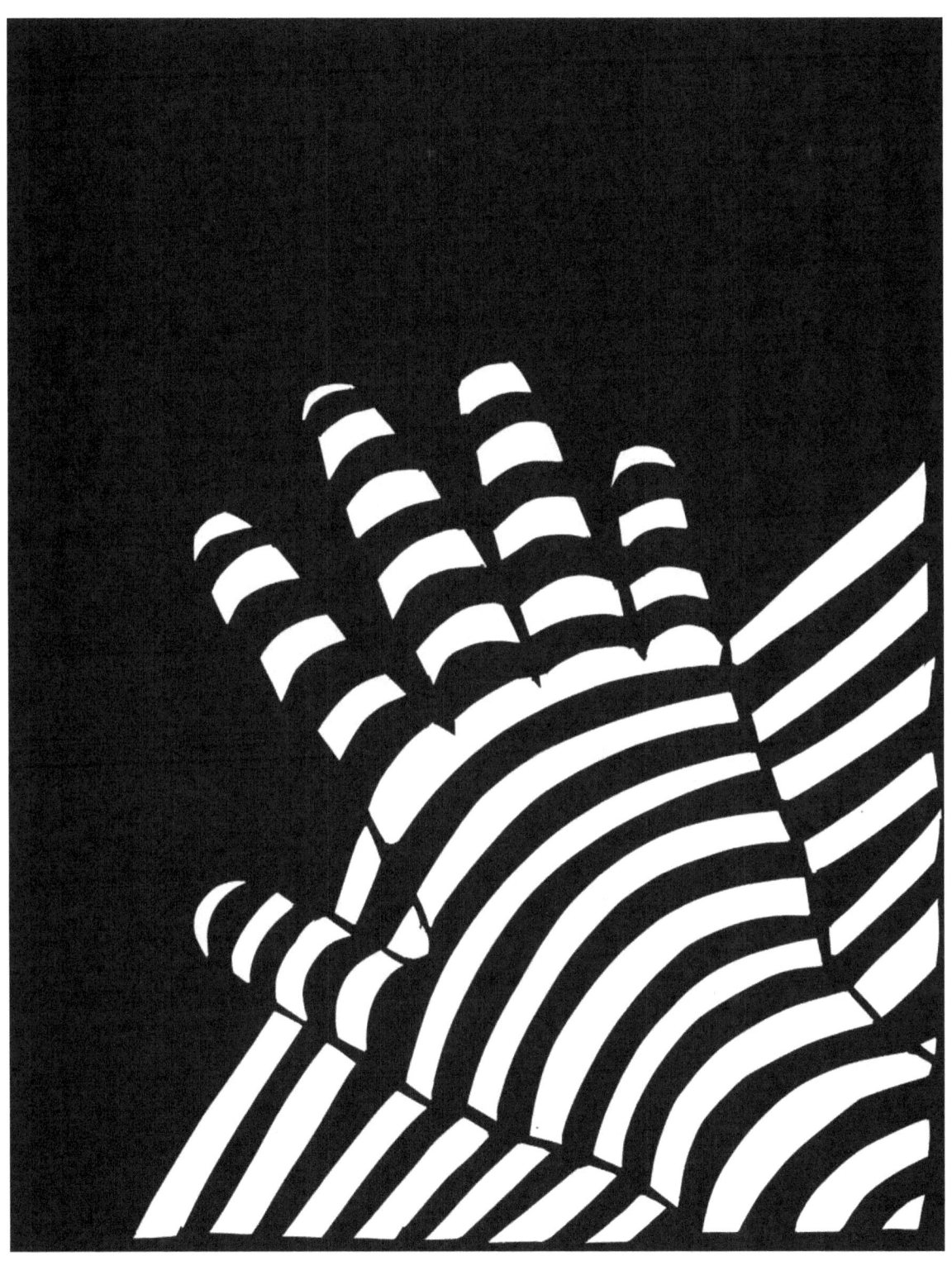

Va'eira *Exodus 6:2-9:35*

God took them from Egypt with a strong hand and an outstretched arm. This story recounts the first few plagues in Egypt, following Pharaoh's refusal to free the Israelites.

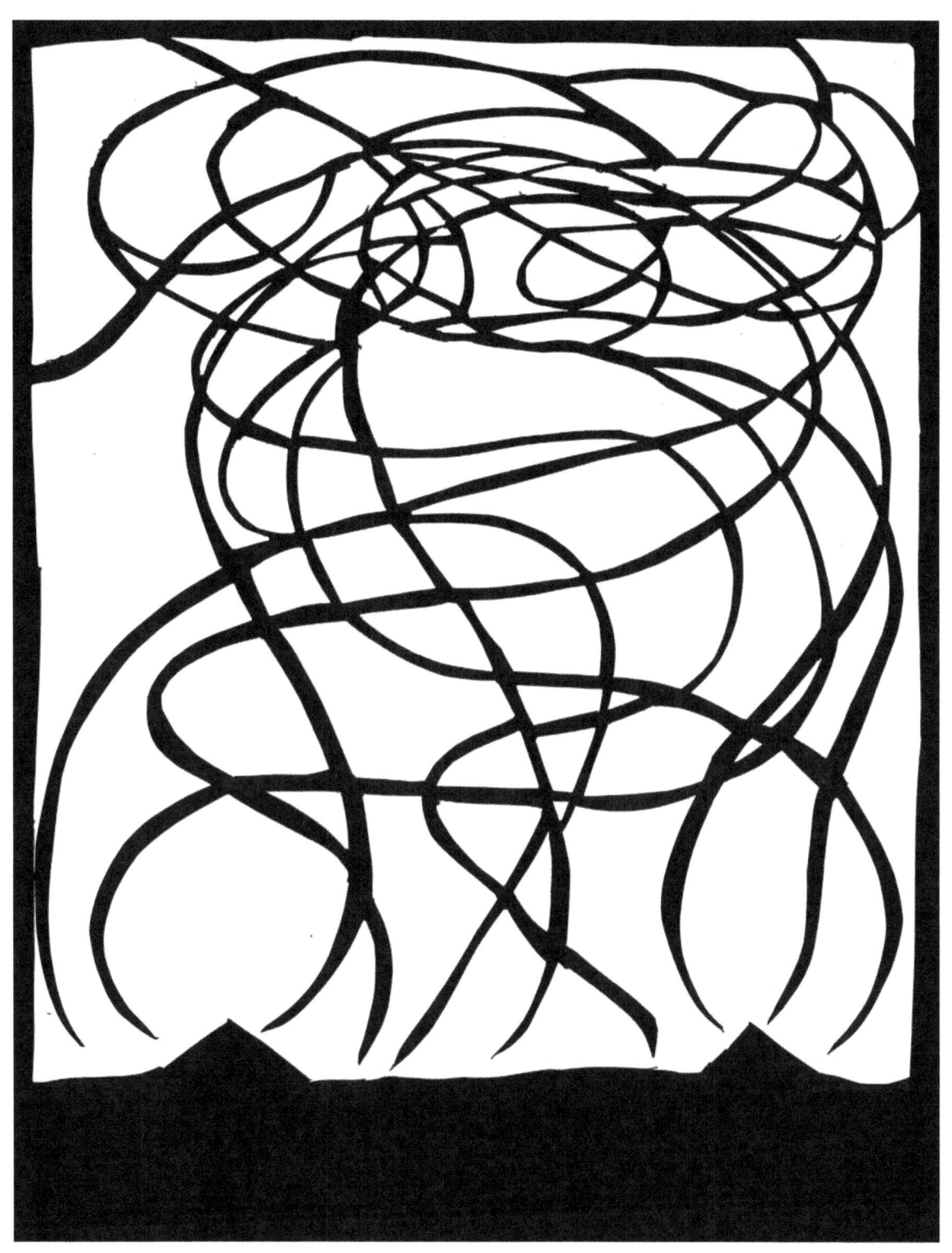

Bo *Exodus 10:1-13:16*

After ten excruciating plagues, Pharaoh finally allows the Israelites to leave Egypt.

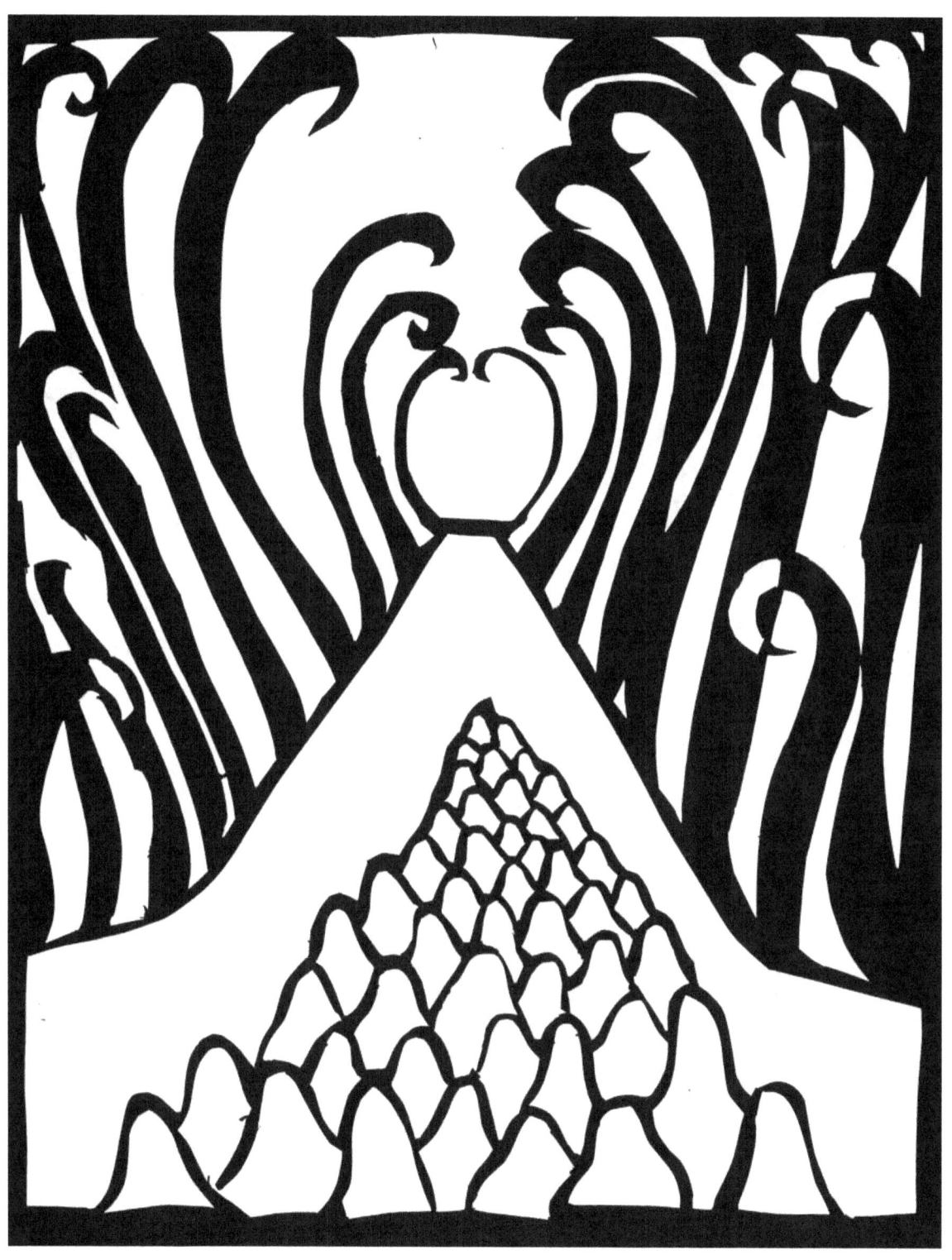

Beshalach *Exodus 13:17–17:16*

The Israelites leave Egypt and are chased by Pharaoh's army, only to arrive at the edge of the Red Sea. This story recounts the splitting of the sea, and their miraculous journey to toward freedom.

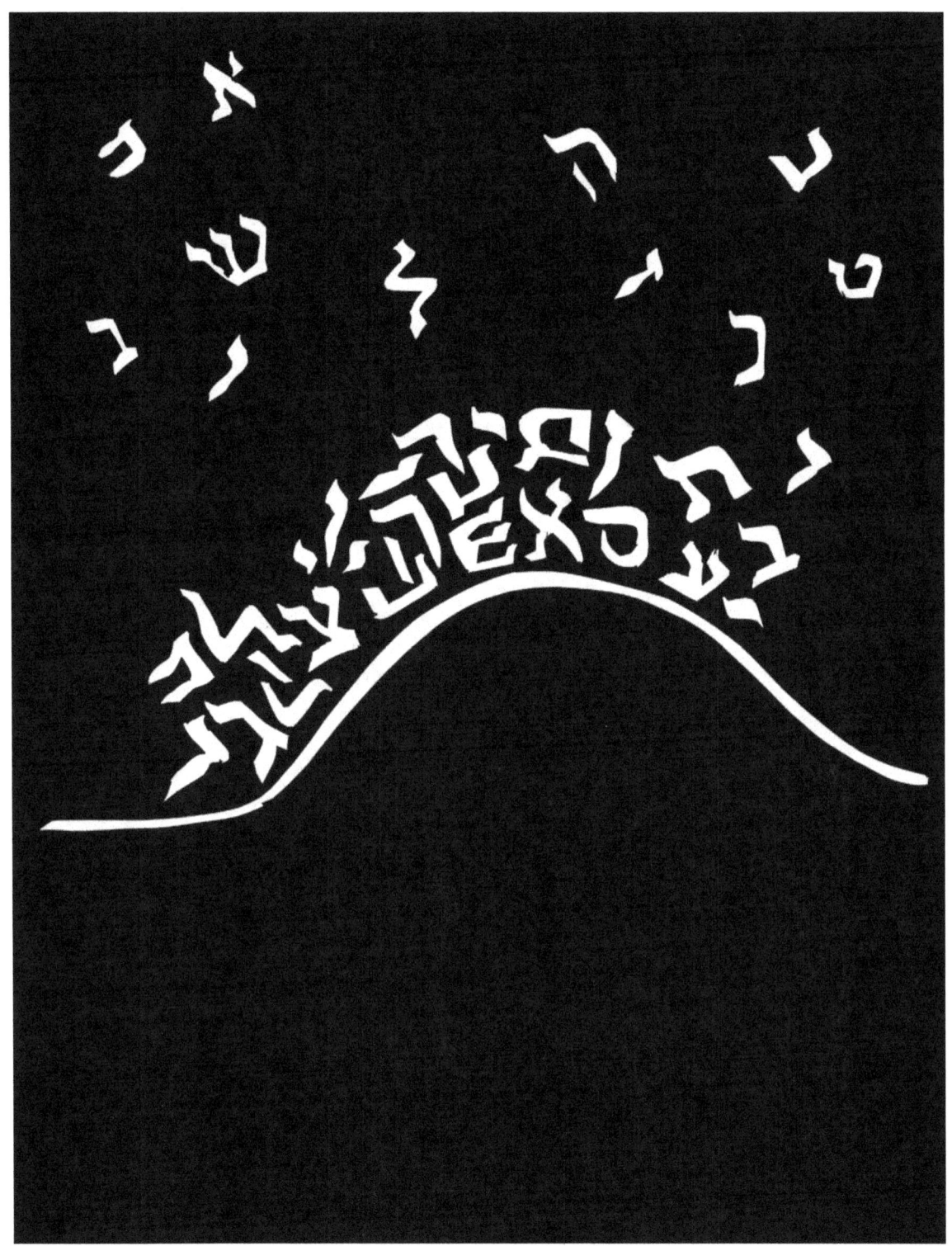

Yitro *Exodus 18:1-20:23*

Forty days after the Israelites arrive in the Sinai desert, they are introduced to the Ten Commandments. The group encounter of God speaking to them from Mount Sinai is represented by Hebrew letters falling from the sky.

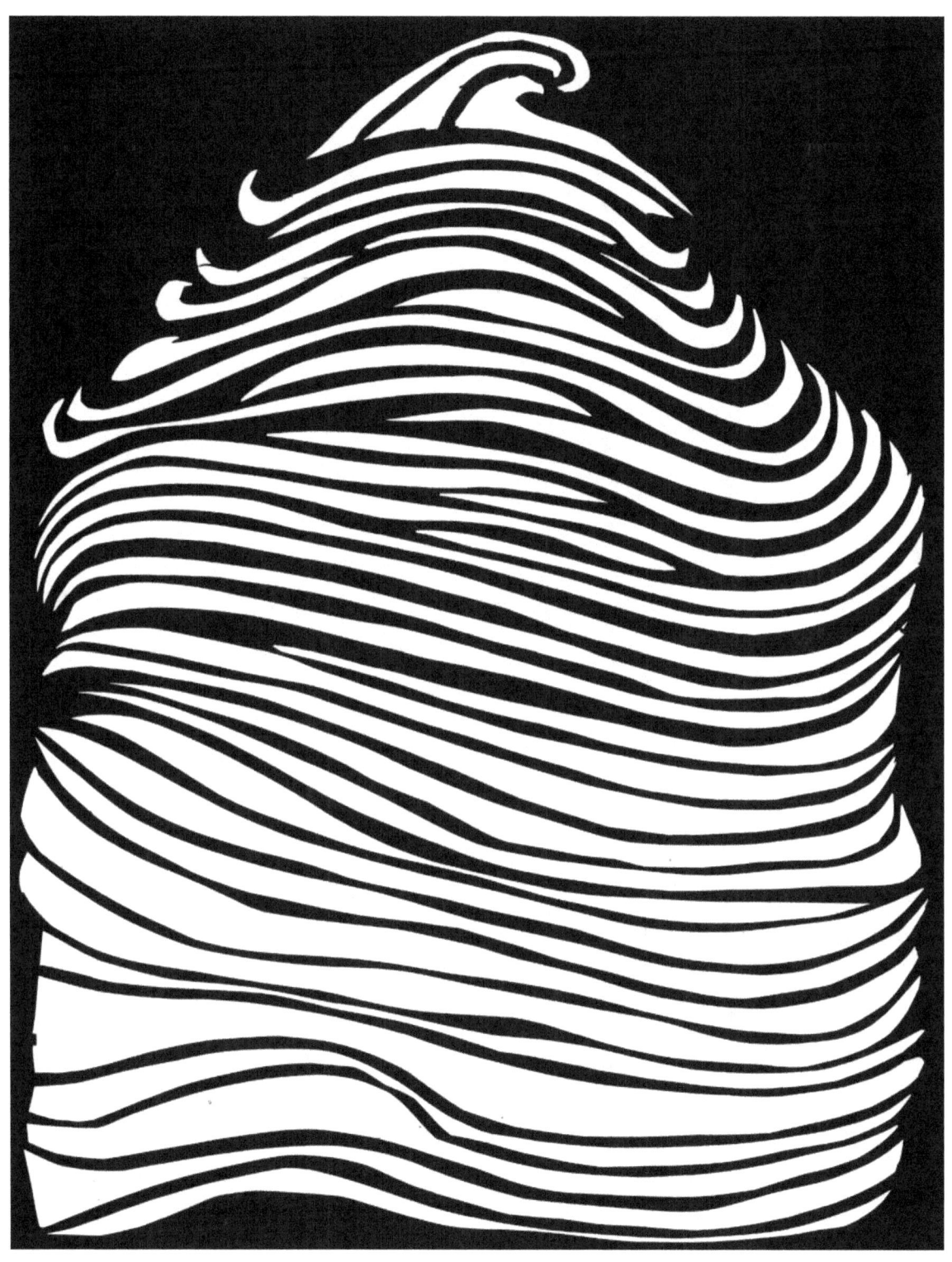

Mishpatim *Exodus 21:1-24:18*

Moses ascends Mount Sinai for forty days to receive the remainder of the commandments, as represented by the forty layers in this image.

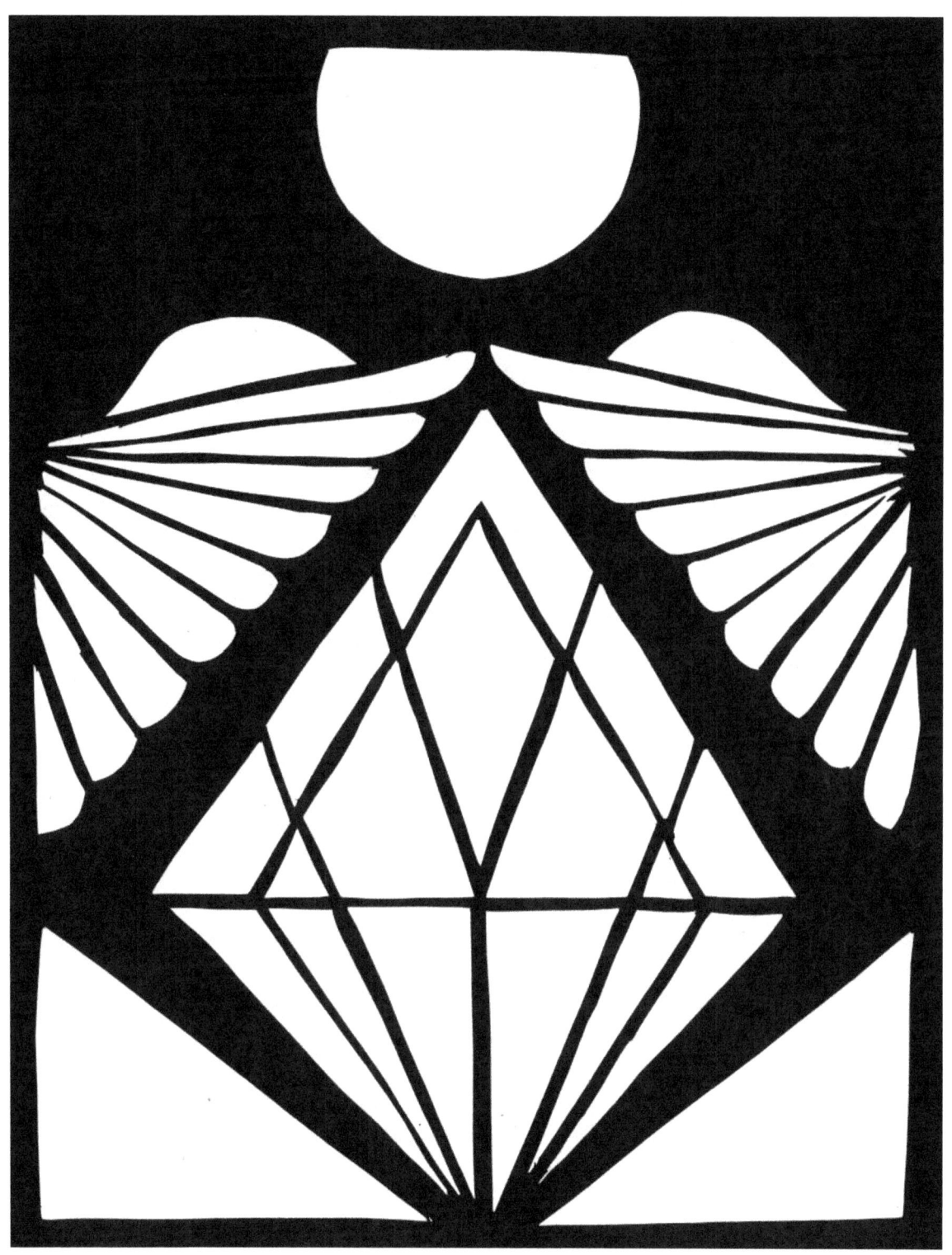

Terumah *Exodus 25:1-27:19*
The Israelites are instructed to build a tabernacle to hold the Tablets. One specification for this structure is to create cherubim on the top, with their wings facing each other.

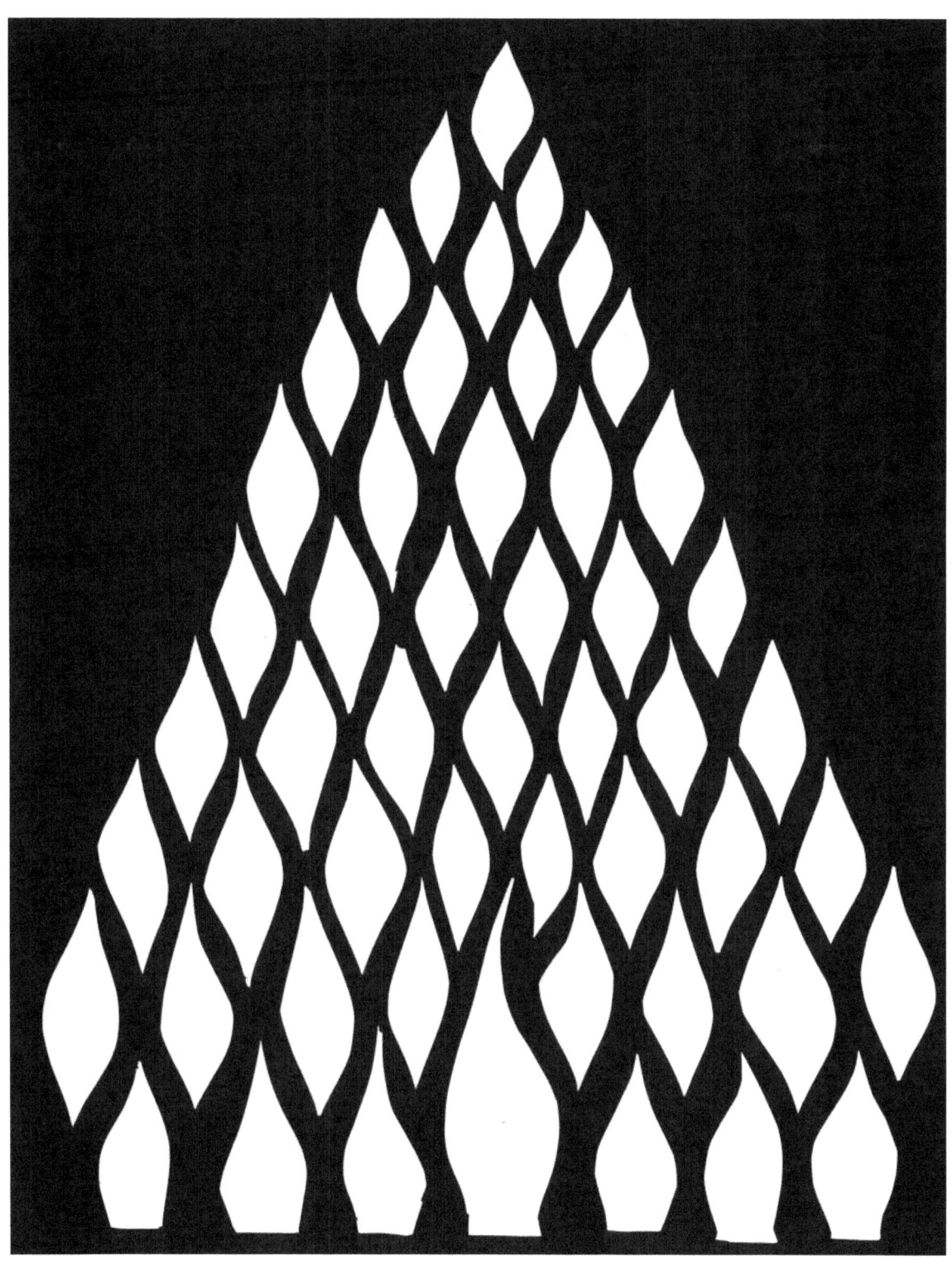

Tetzaveh *Exodus 27:20-30:10*

Details of the Tabernacle include creating a seven branched candelabra. The seven flames at the bottom of the image evolve into eight (a hint of Hanukkah), and eventually reach the top with one flame representing unity and oneness.

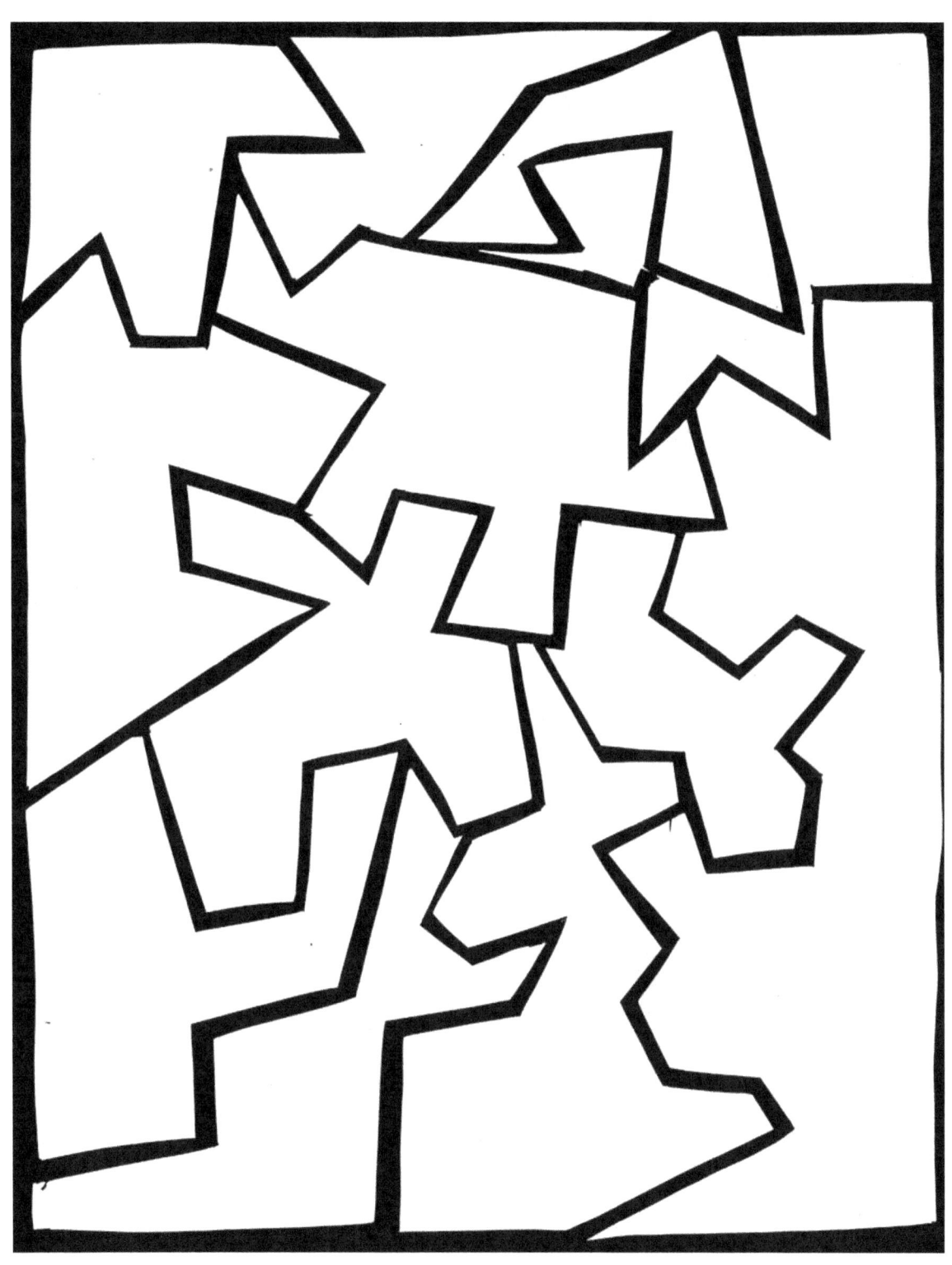

Ki Tisa *Exodus 30:11-34:35*

This story recounts Moses descending Mt. Sinai, and observing his followers praying to a golden calf. He throws the Tablets on the ground, and they shatter into multiple pieces. In this same section, readers are also introduced to the thirteen attributes of God.

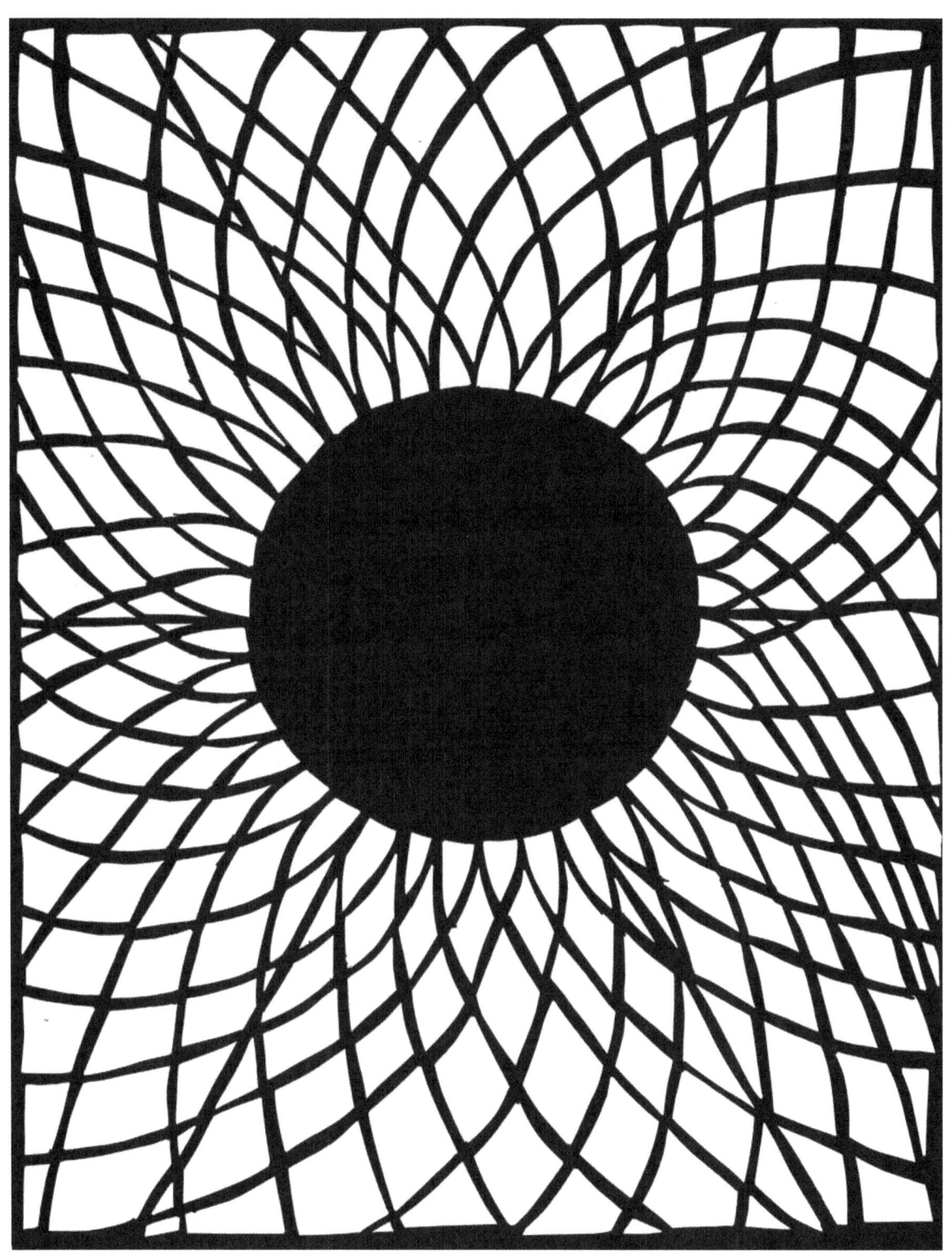

Vayakhel *Exodus 35:1-38:20*

Moses instructs the Israelites on the laws of the Sabbath. This imagery represents the Sabbath as the circle in the center, with six sections radiating outward, representing the days of the week. In this weekly cycle, the Sabbath impacts all of the days of the week.

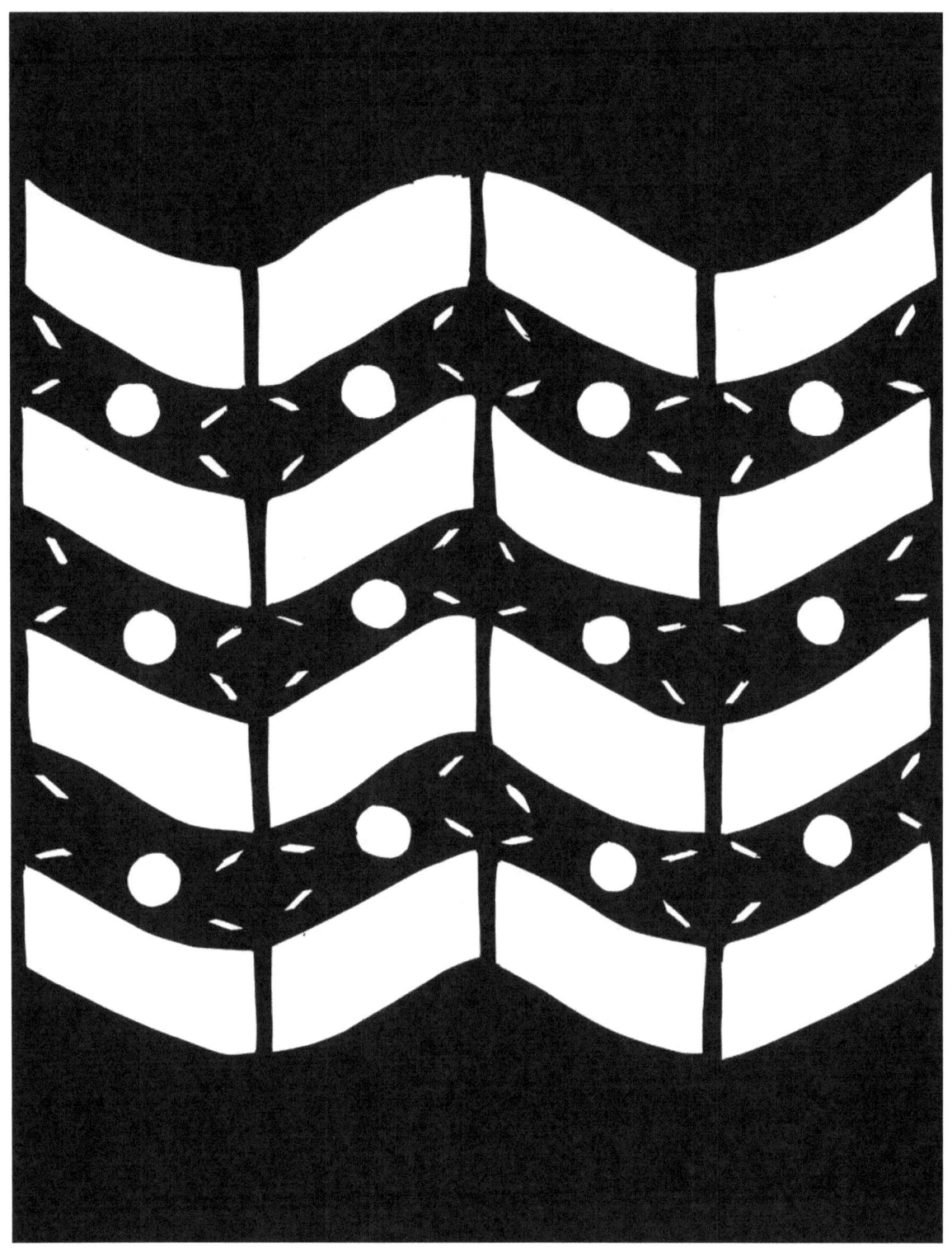

Pekudei *Exodus 38:21-40:38*

The high priests are instructed to wear specific garments during their rituals. This image is a variation of the priestly breastplate, set with twelve precious stones to represent each tribe.

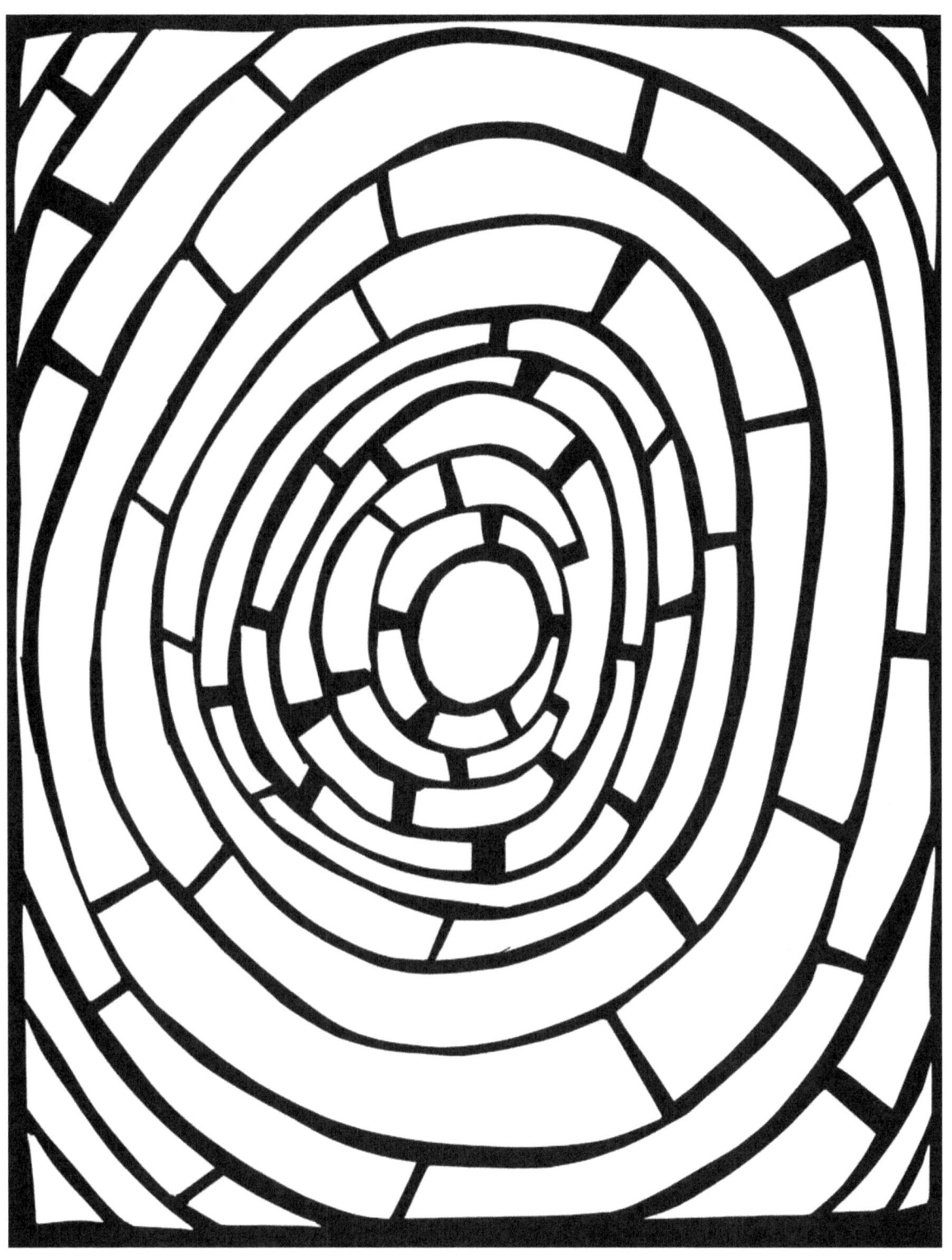

Vayikra *Leviticus 1:1–5:26*
Much of this story relates to the laws of animal sacrifices. The concentric circles represent the tribes living and working together in harmony as they adjust to a life of freedom.

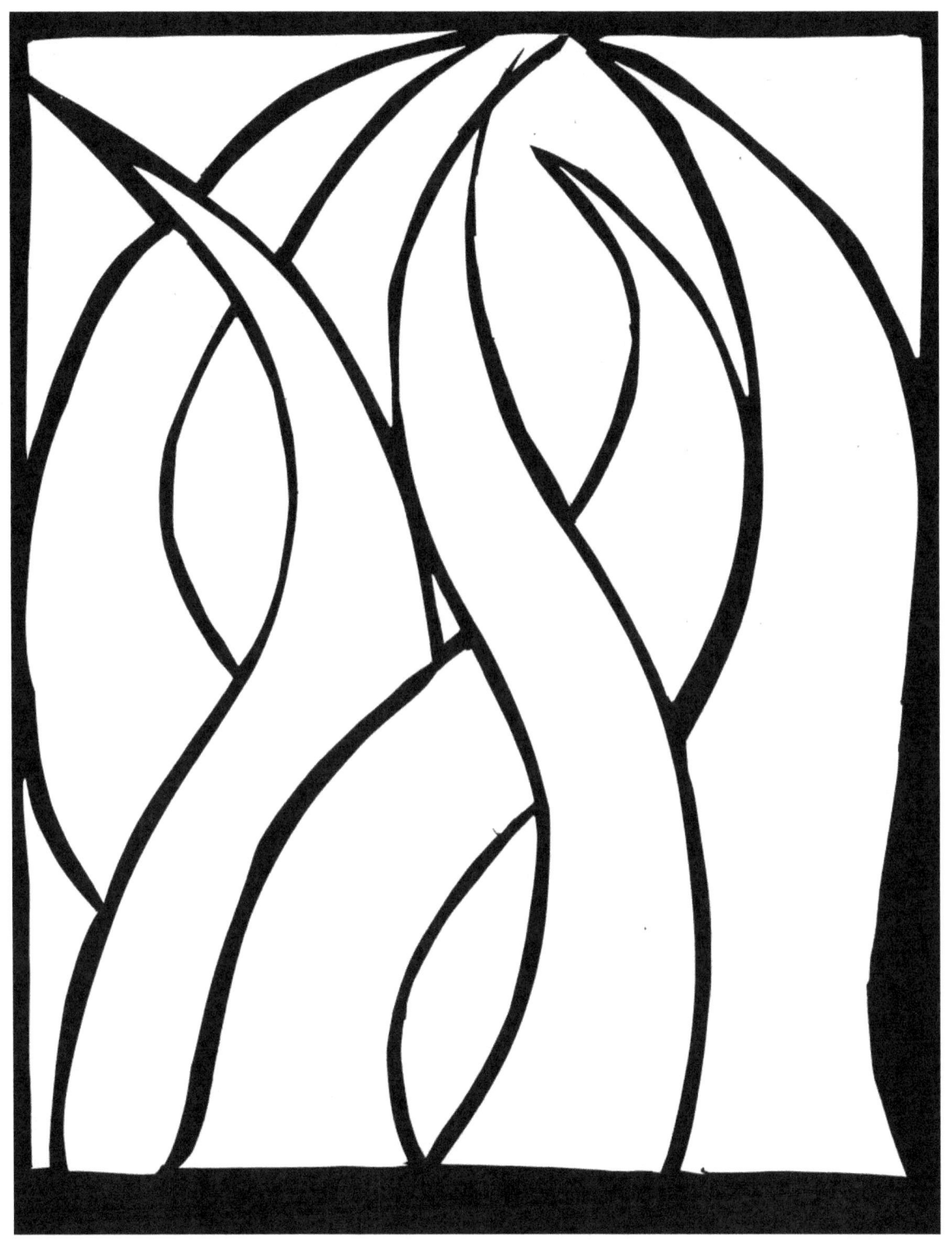

Tzav *Leviticus 6:1-8:36*

Sacrifices are a part of daily life of ancient Israelites, and a continuous fire on the altar is required to fulfill their rituals.

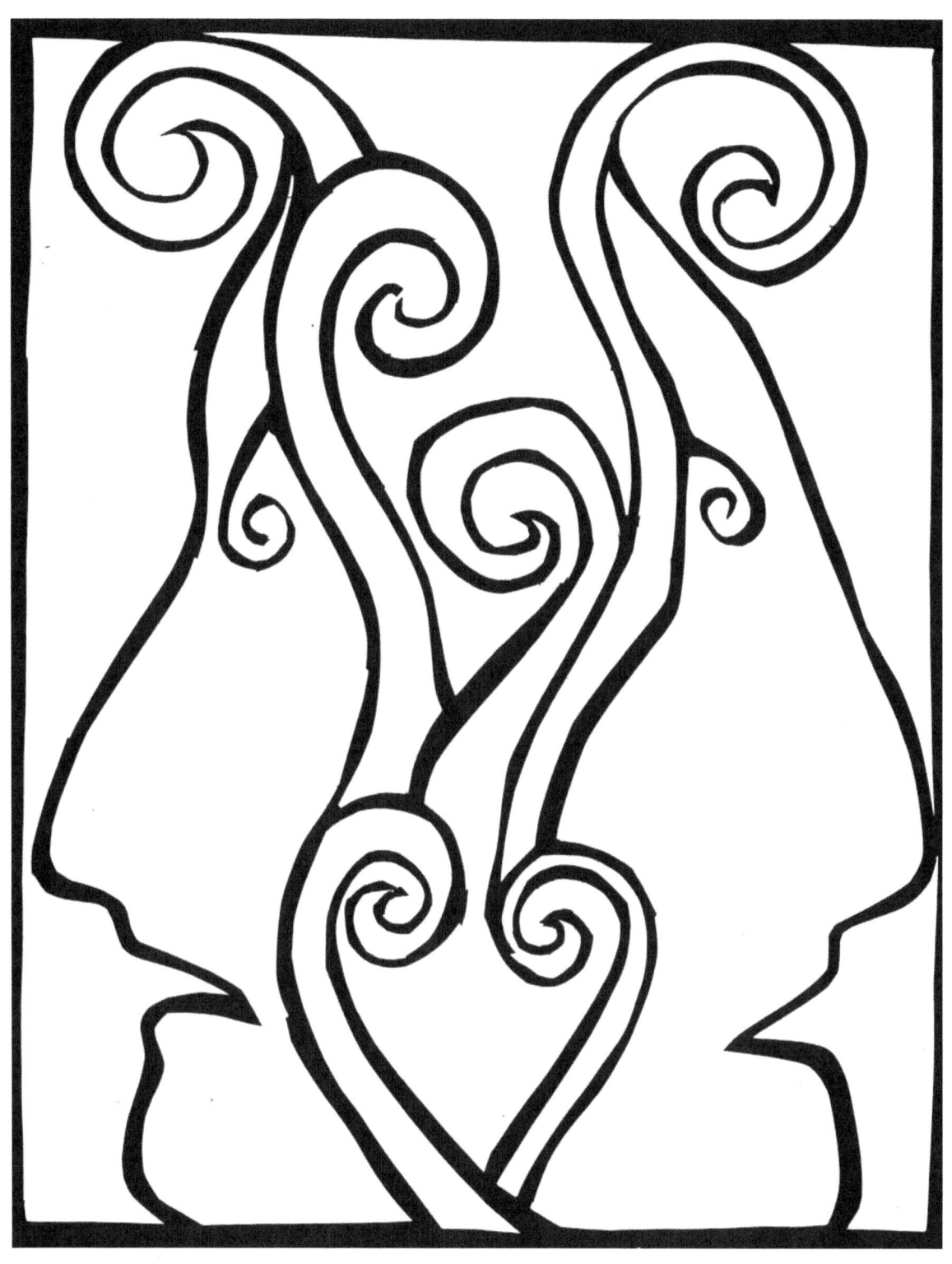

Shemini *Leviticus 9:1–11:47*

Nadav and Avihu, the sons of Aaron, attempt to go above and beyond their allocated duties to please God. Their offering of *strange fire* results in their untimely deaths.

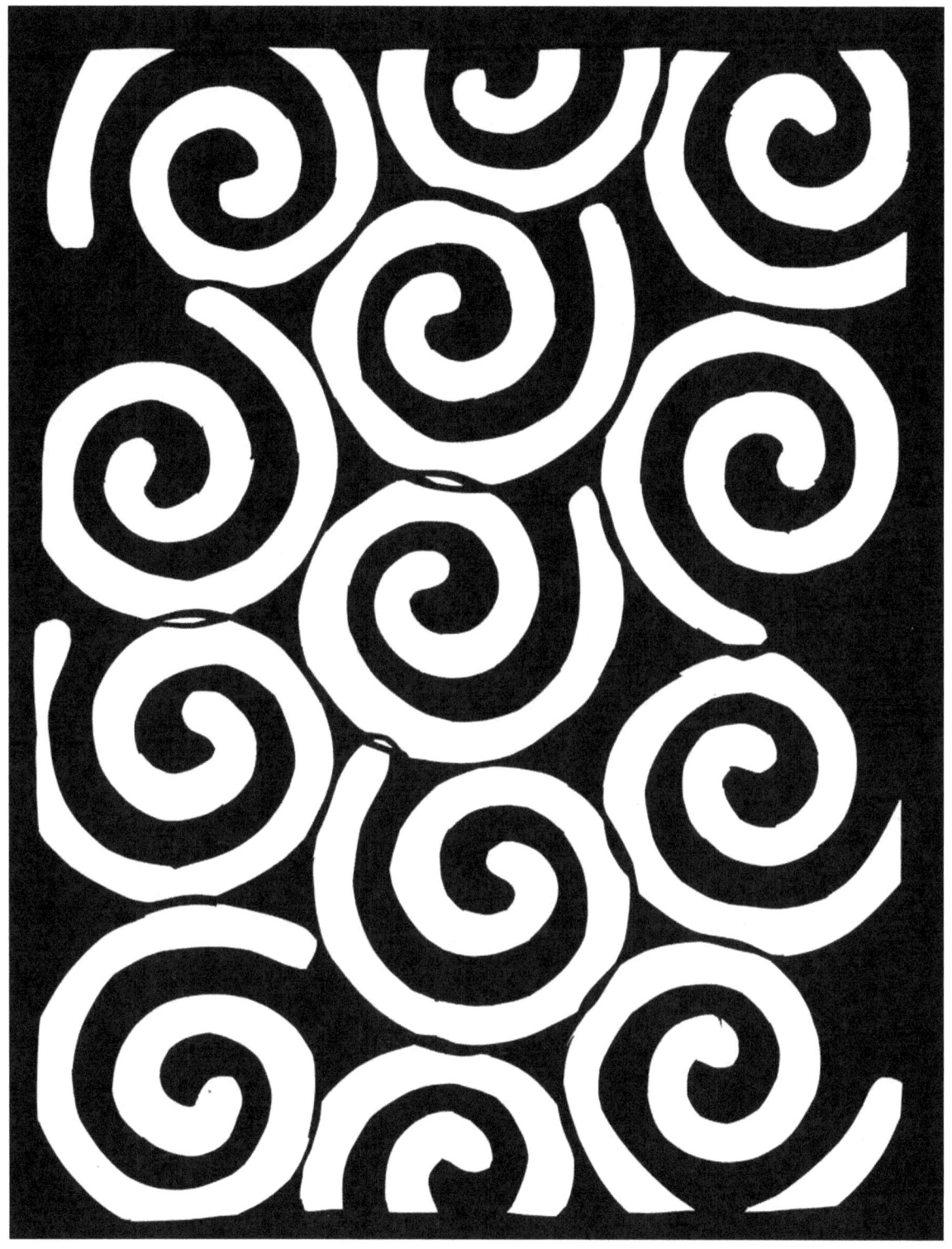

Tazria *Leviticus 12:1-13:59*

"Tzaraat", introduced in this story as something best described as *spiritual leprosy*, is a spiritual plague brought on by the spreading of gossip.

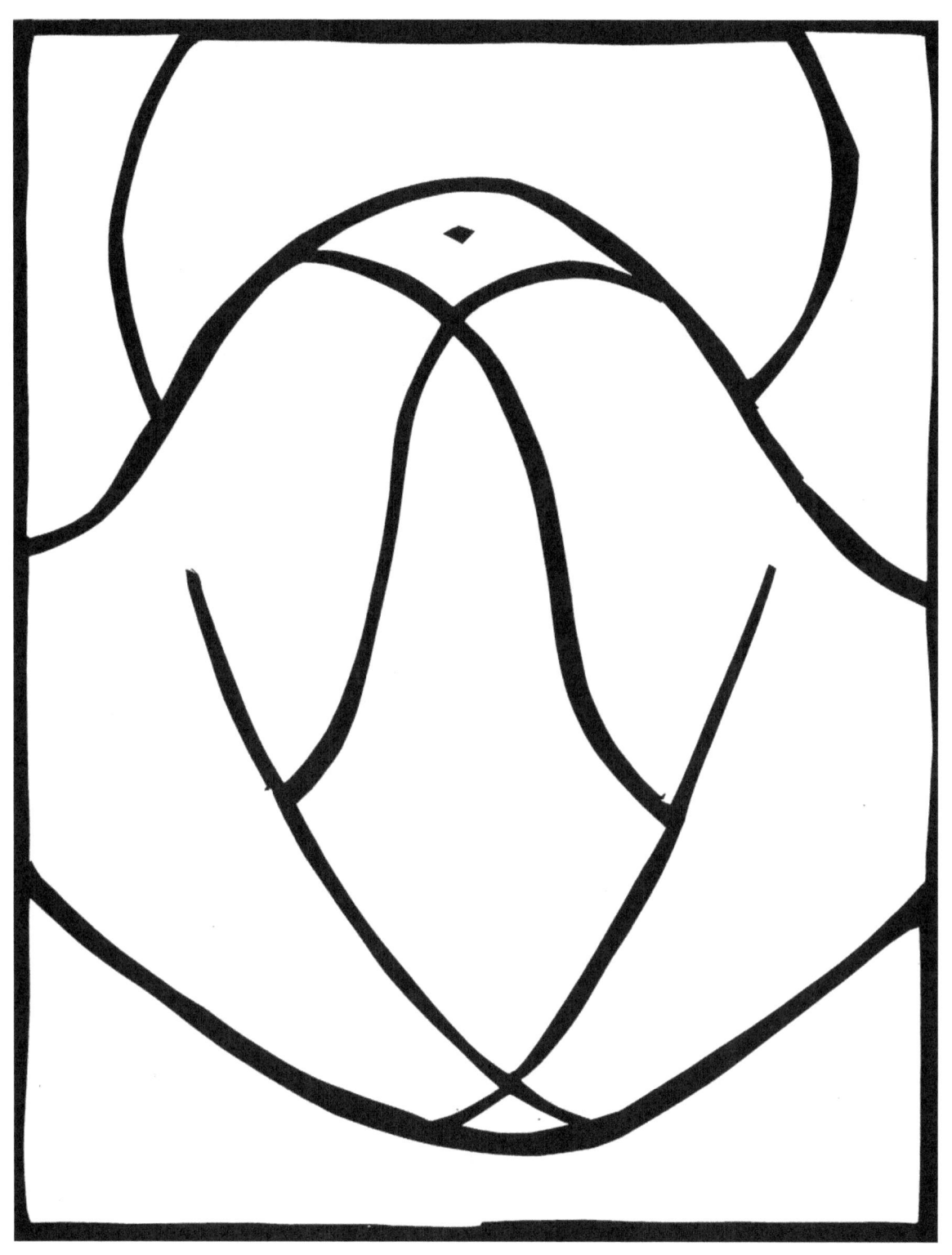

Metzora *Leviticus 14:1–15:33*
One part of the recipe to alleviate *spiritual leprosy* involved a ceremony using two birds.

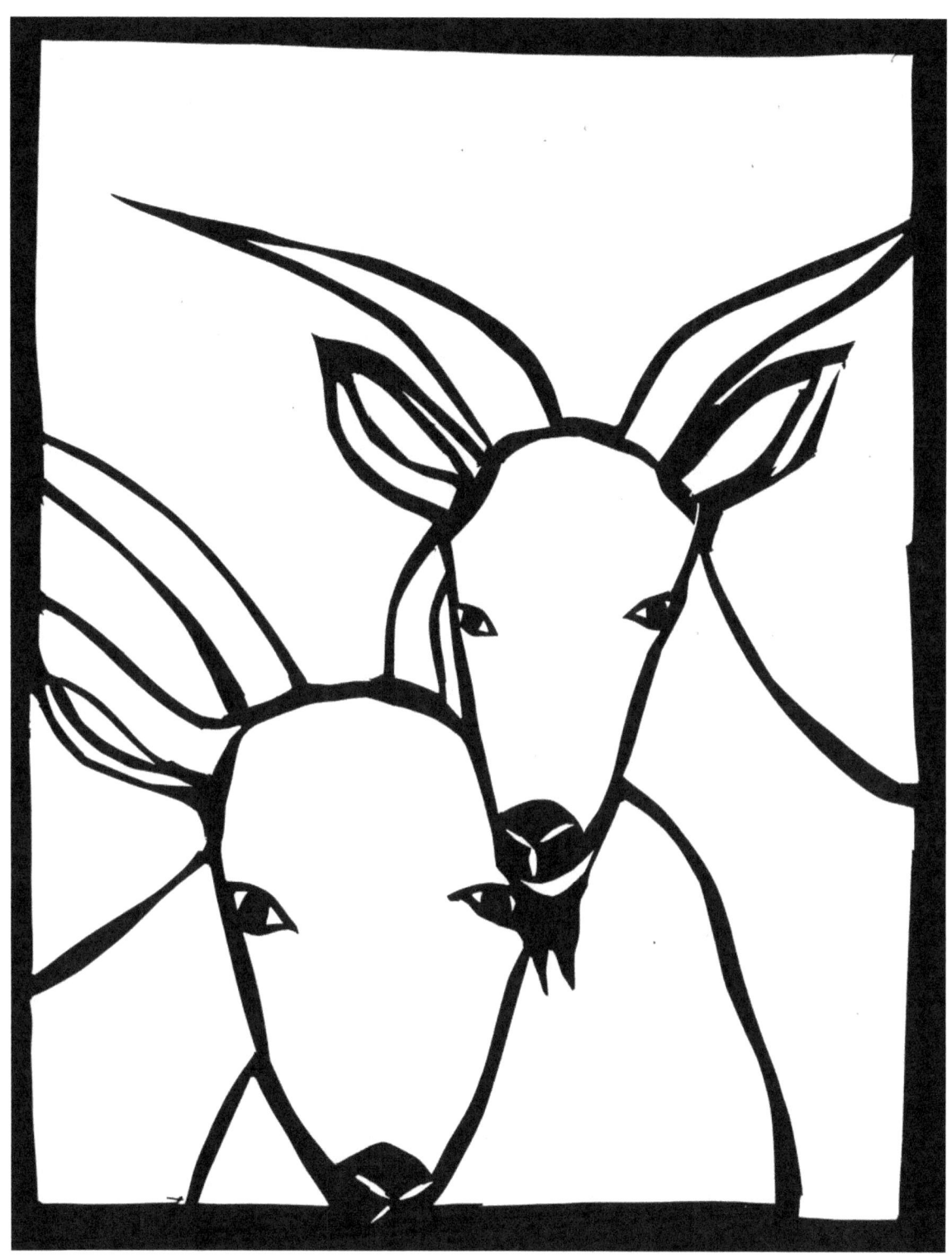

Acharei *Leviticus 16:1–18:30*

Animals were often used to sublimate the Israelites' sins through sacrifice and other means, as highlighted throughout the Torah. In this story, two goats are described in the ritual, and serve as the basis for the Day of Atonement.

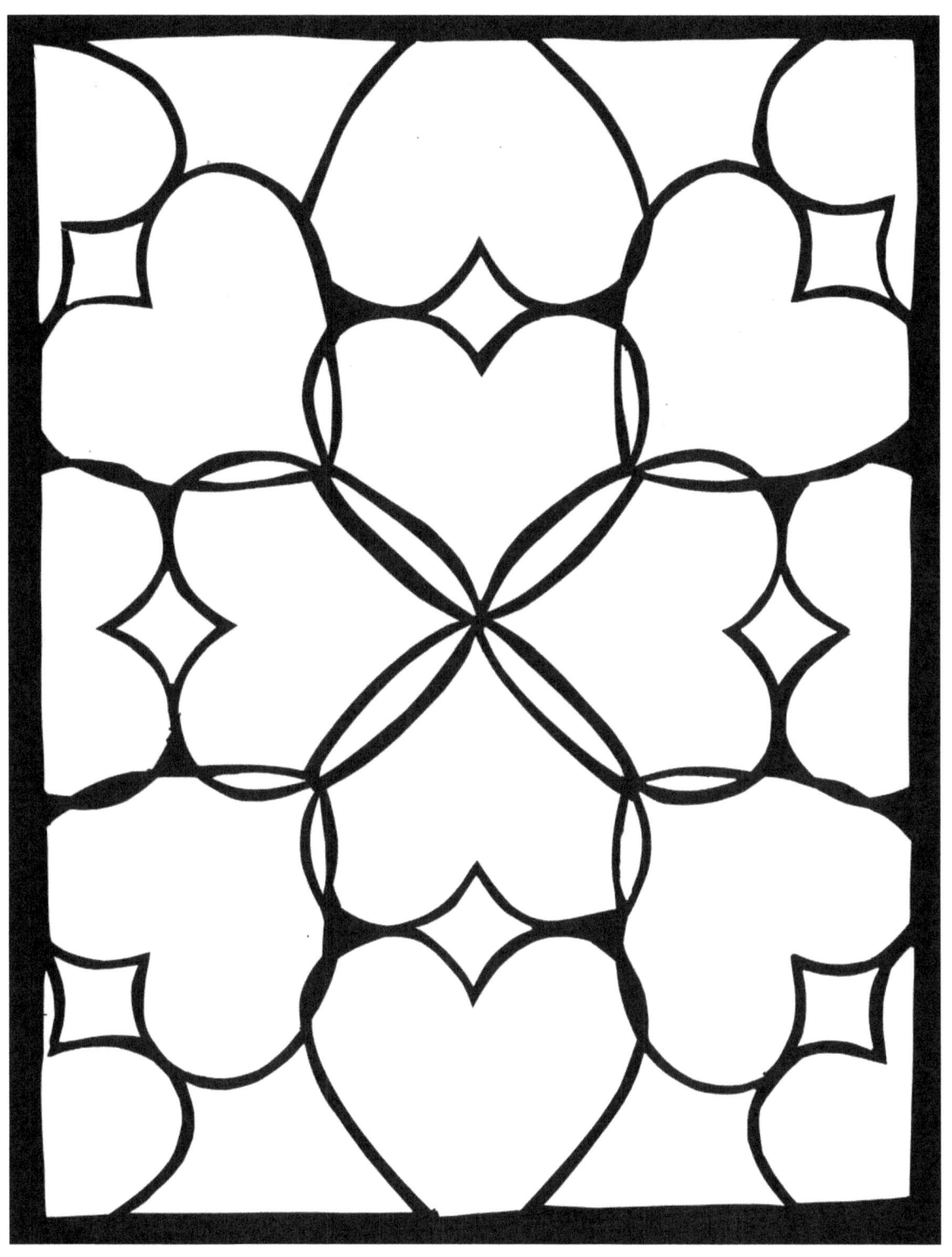

Kedoshim *Leviticus 19:1–20:27*

Love your neighbor as yourself is a famous idea highlighted in this story. Some say the entire Hebrew Bible can be summed up in this idea, and the rest is commentary.

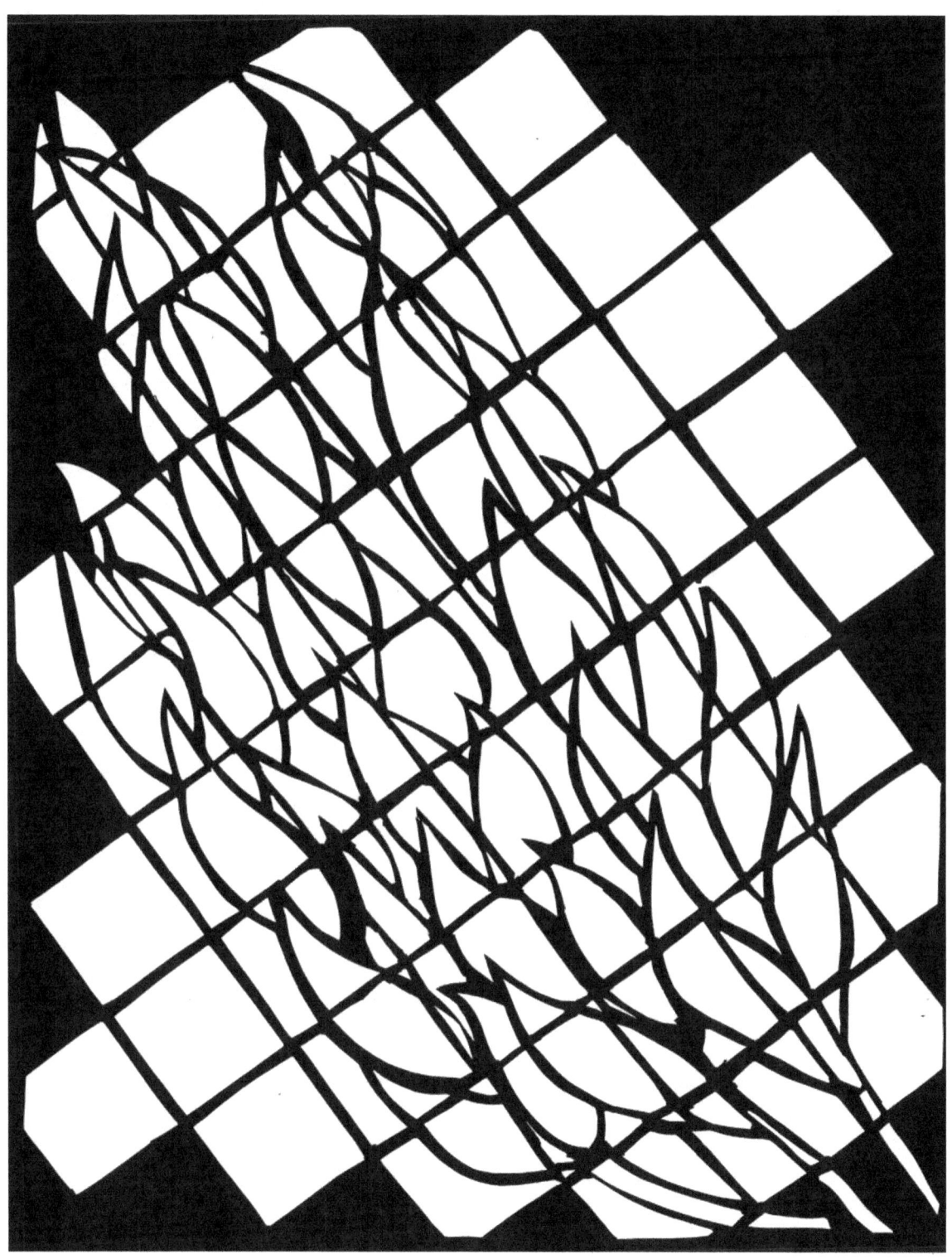

Emor *Leviticus 21:1–24:23*

Shavuot celebrates the 49 days between the Israelites' departure from Egypt and the receiving of the Torah, as represented in this image with 49 squares. The counting during this time period also corresponded to the ancient barley harvest.

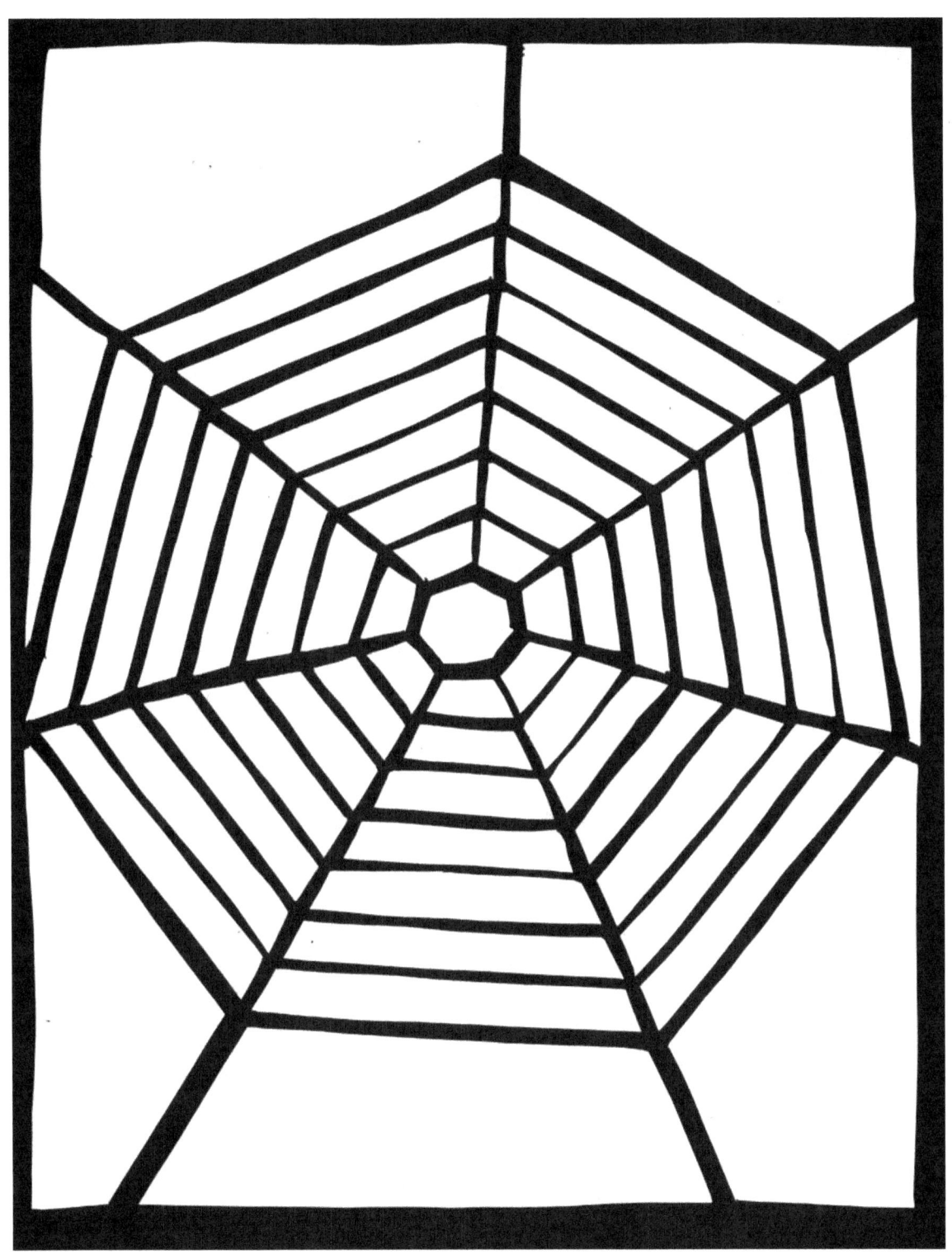

Behar *Leviticus 25:1-26:2*

This story introduces the agricultural laws of letting the land lay fallow every seven years. The jubilee year, occurred every 50 years, and served as a time for all of the land to rest. The imagery represents crops divided up into seven groups of seven, with the 50th year in the center.

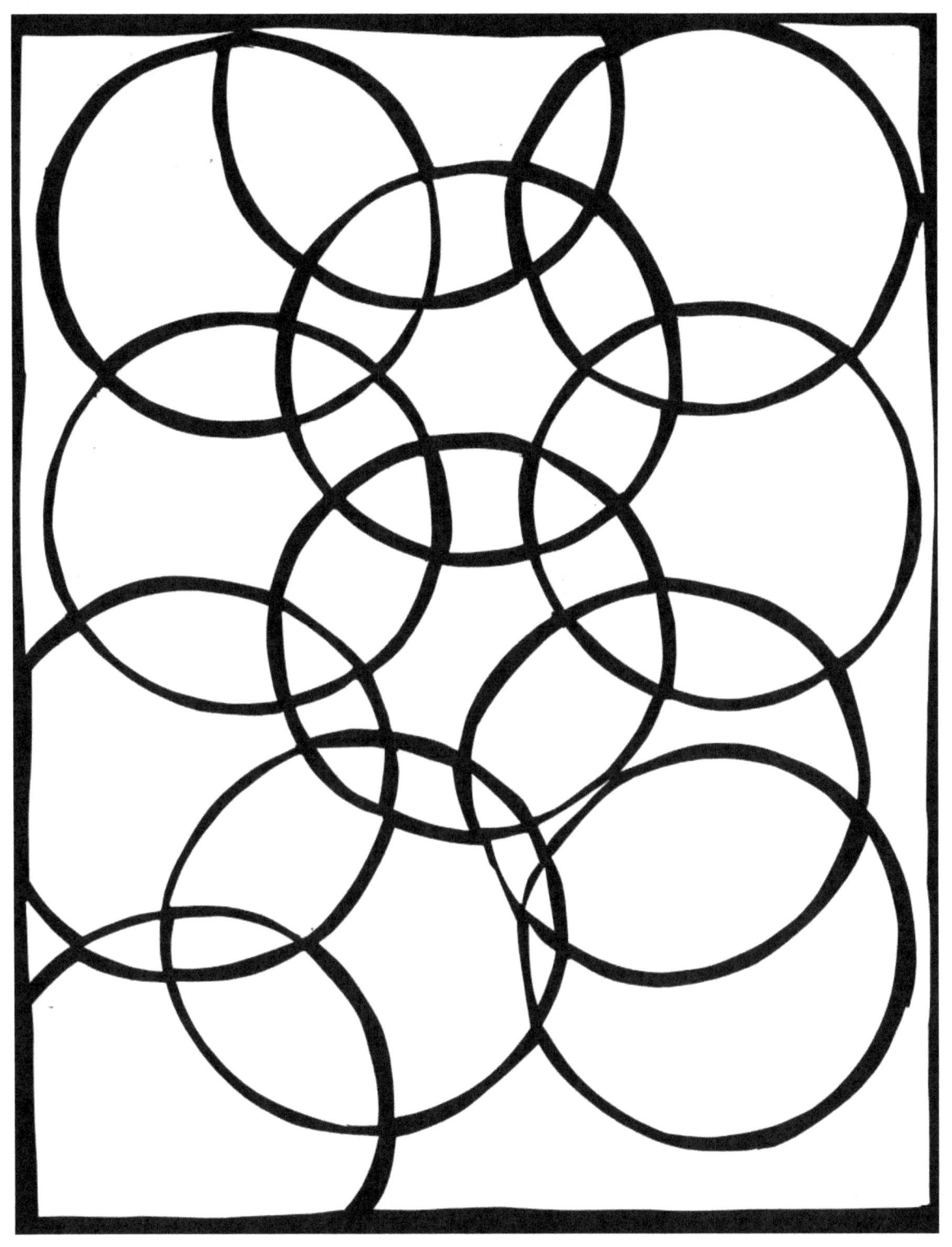

Bechukotai *Leviticus 26:3-27:34*
God makes a promise to the Israelites that they will experience material wealth and prosperity if they follow his commandments.

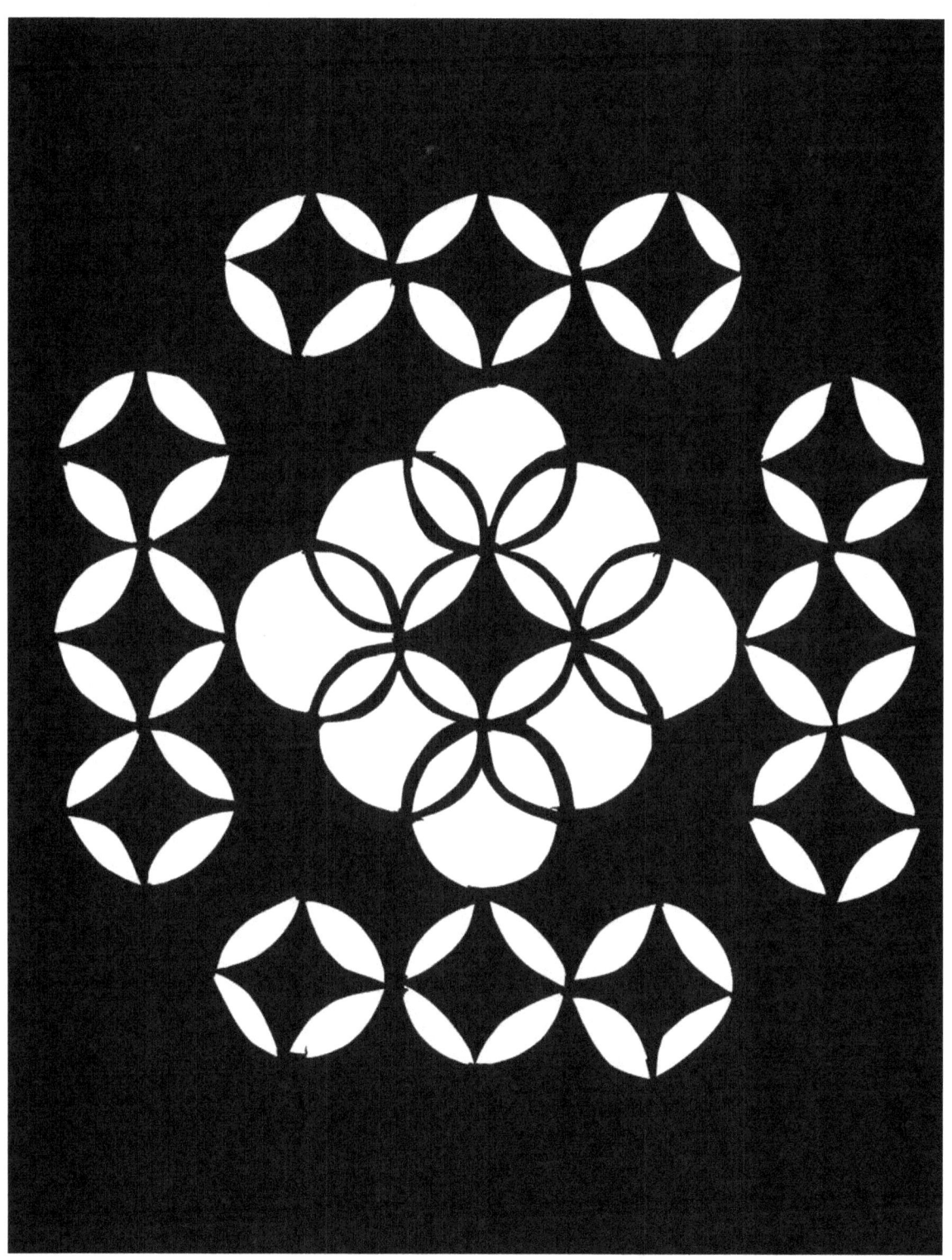

Bamidbar *Numbers 1:1–4:20*
The twelve tribes were organized around the tabernacle, and each camp had a flag corresponding to their tribe.

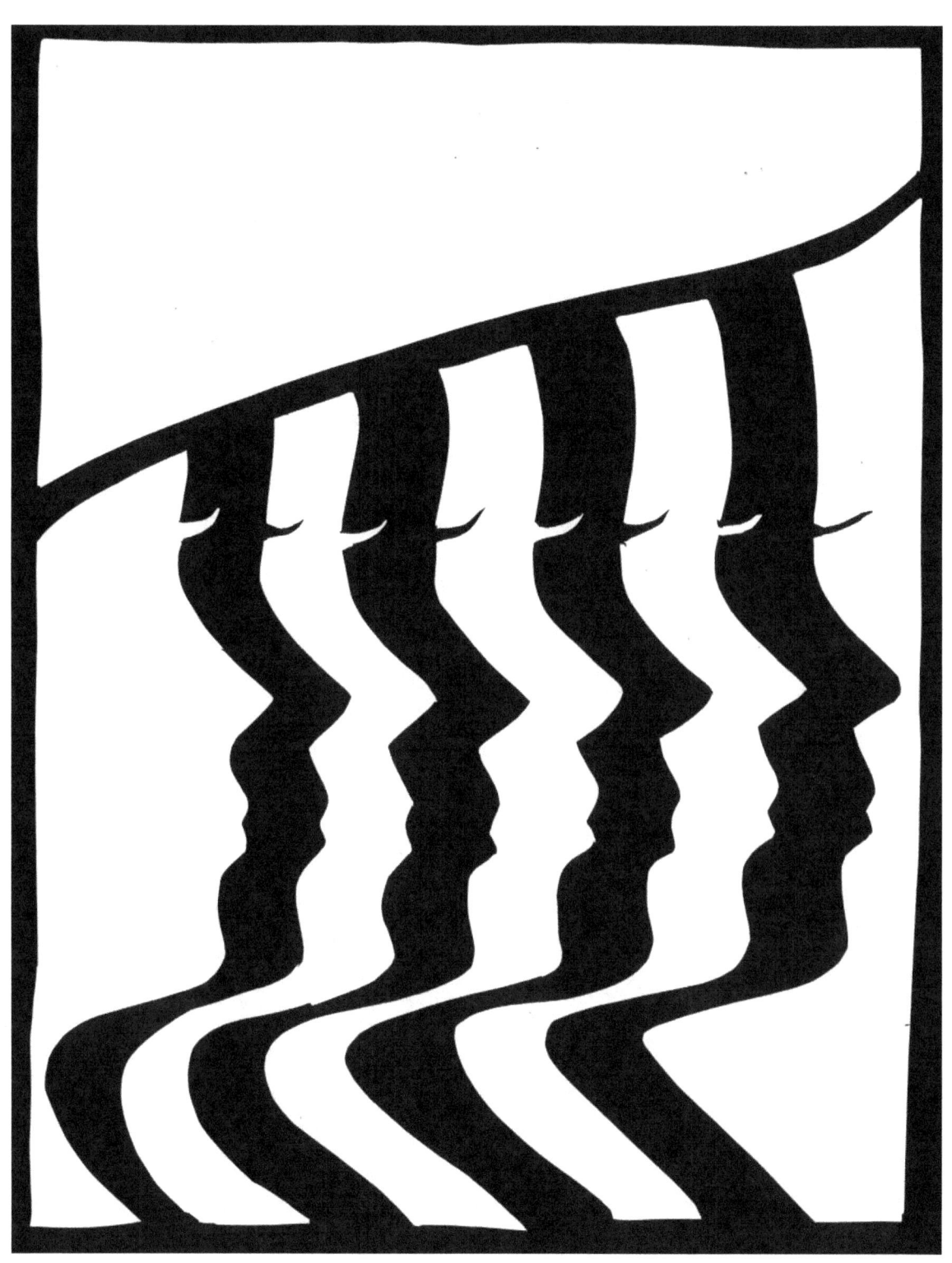

Naso *Numbers 4:21–7:89*

This story describes the complicated status and punishment of a wayward wife. Rabbinical sources explain the practice actually highlighted the ethical behavior of the Israelite women.

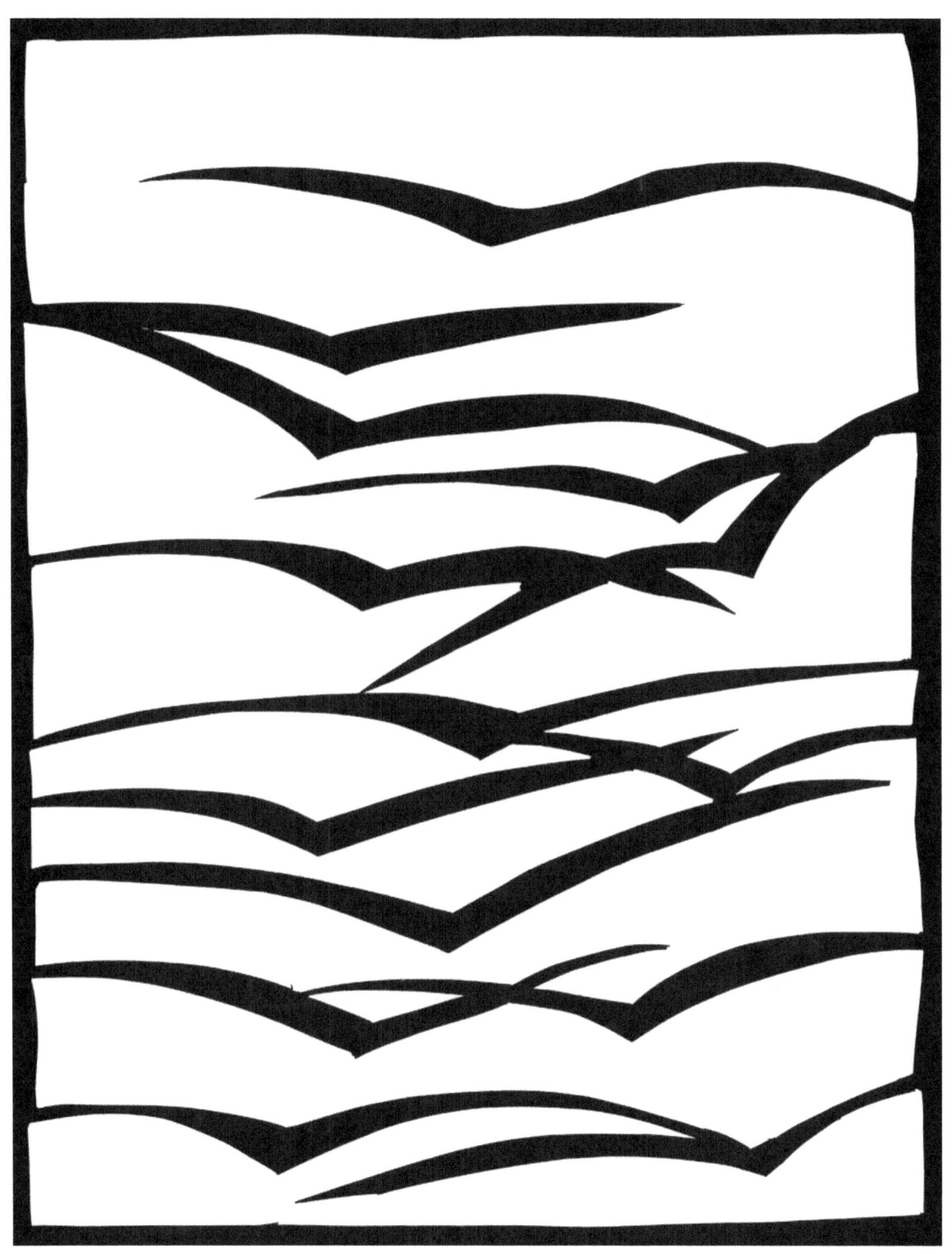

Behaalotecha *Numbers 8:1–12:16*

This story recounts the Israelites' complaints about their daily manna sustenance, and their desire for meat. Moses intervenes and asks for a flock of birds to be sent into the desert.

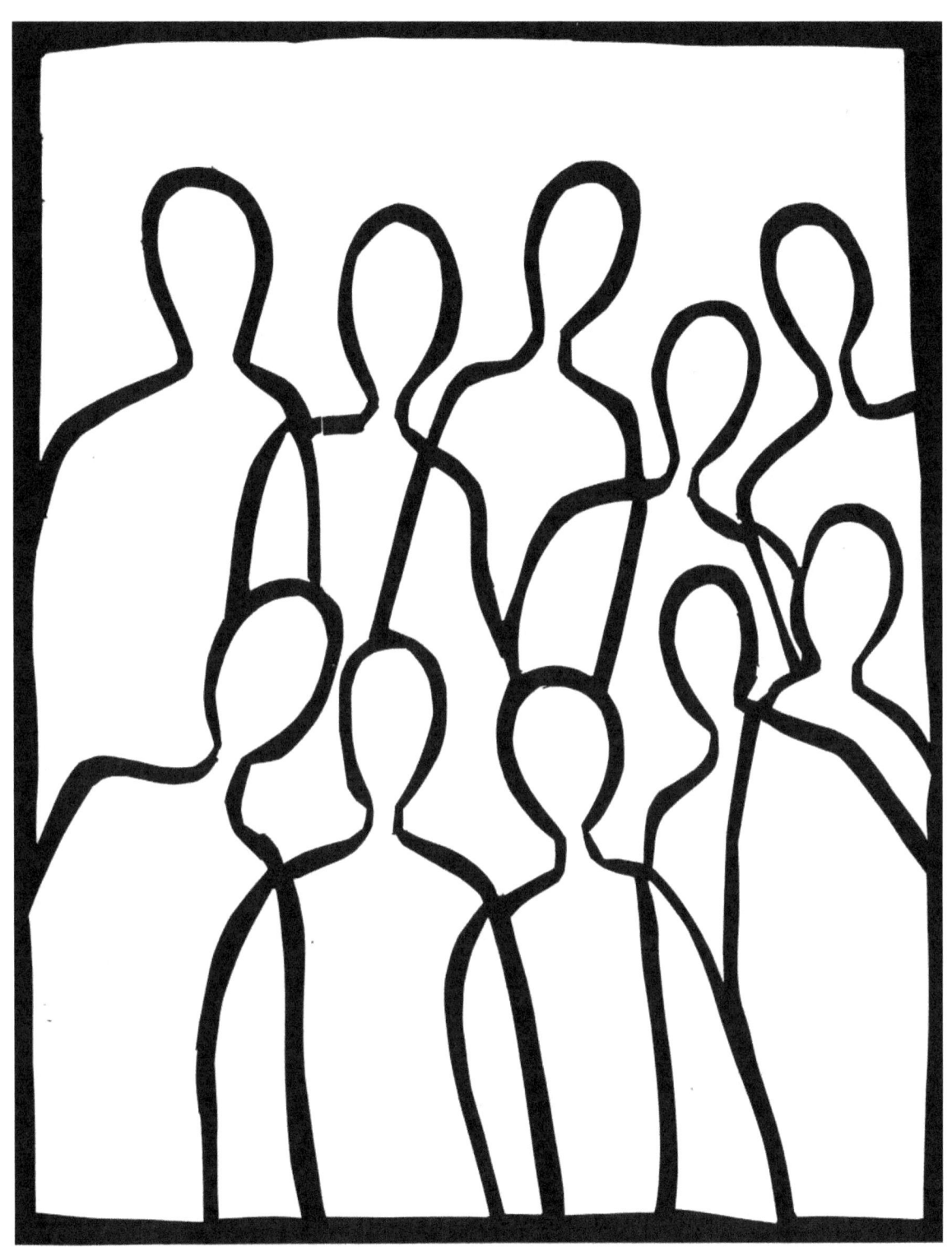

Shelach *Numbers 13:1–15:41*

The Israelites send twelve spies into Israel to explore the land they will inhabit. Ten of the spies return with a negative report. The punishment for this negative attitude results in the postponement of entering the land. For forty years, the Israelites will wander around the desert.

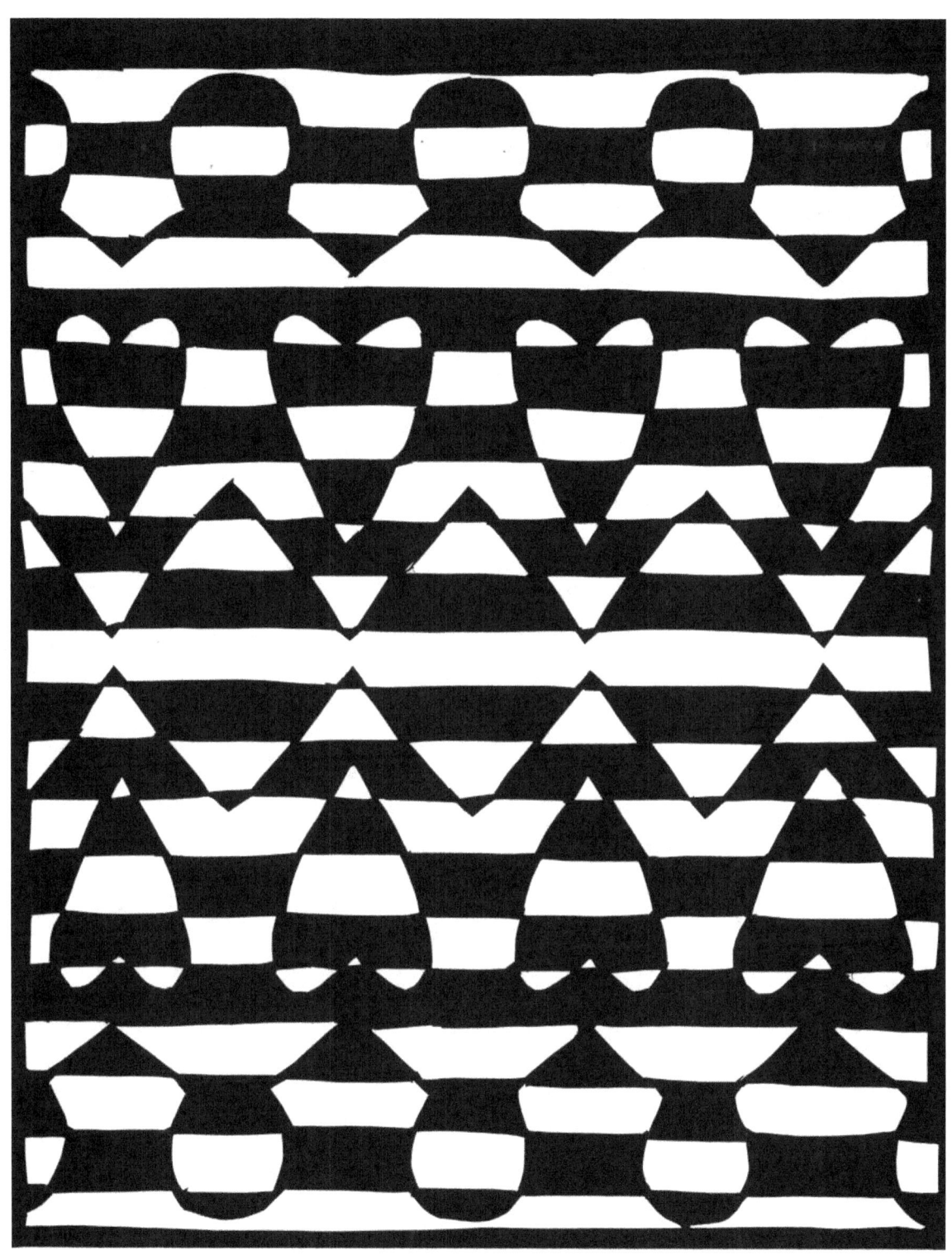

Korach *Numbers 16:1–18:32*

Moses' wealthy cousin Korach questions Moses' power, and initiates a rebellion to challenge his leadership. The uprising results in the earth swallowing Korach and his followers.

Chukat *Numbers 19:1–22:1*

Following the death of Miriam, the Israelites complain to Moses, begging him for water. Moses is instructed to tap a rock, but chooses instead to angrily hit it with force. His punishment for the transgression prevents him from entering the Promised Land.

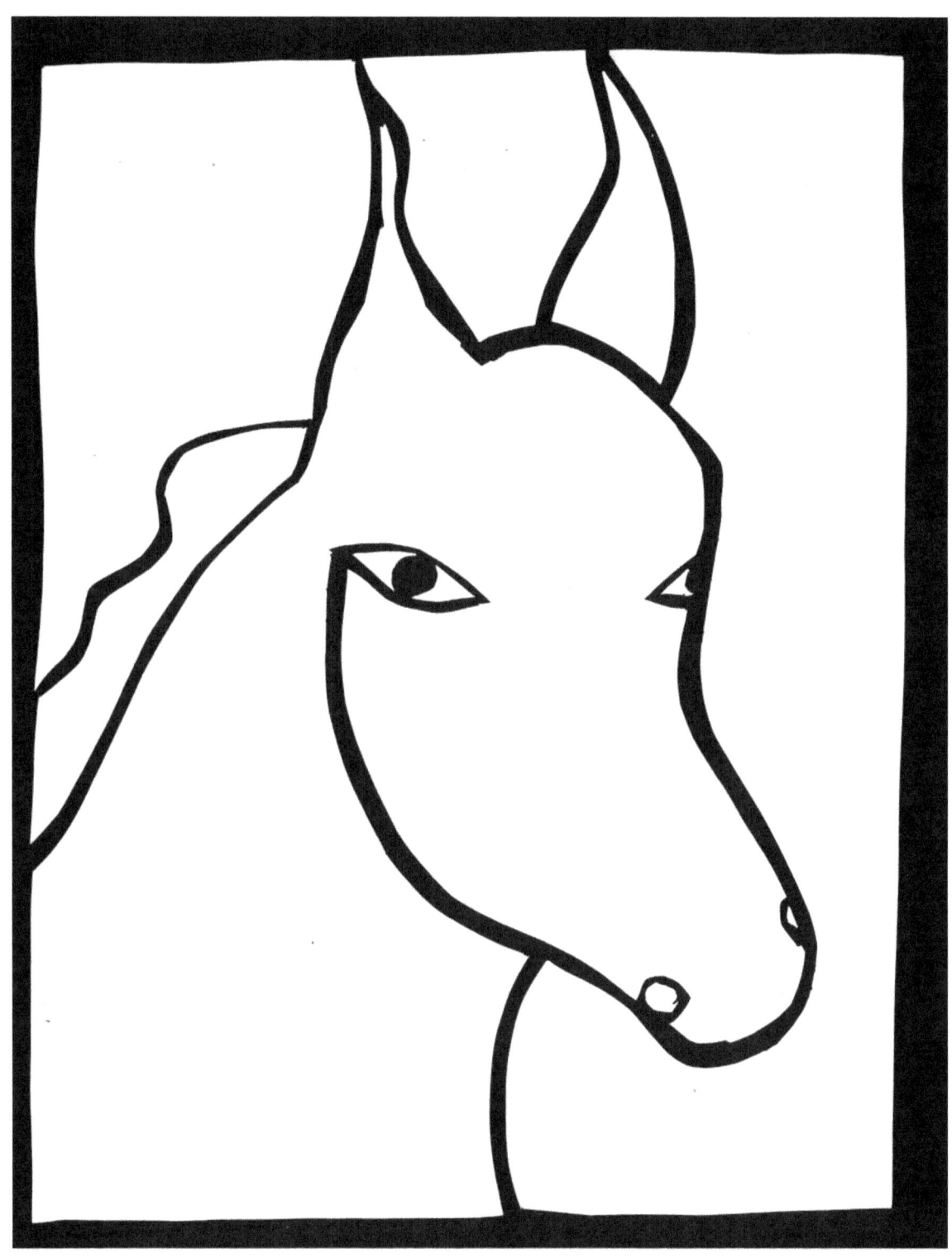

Balak *Numbers 22:2–25:9*

This unusual story involves a man named Balaam who sets out to curse the Israelites, on behalf of the Moabite king, Balak. Three different times, his donkey blocks the way, sensing an angel in the path. Balaam is forced to give a blessing to the Israelites.

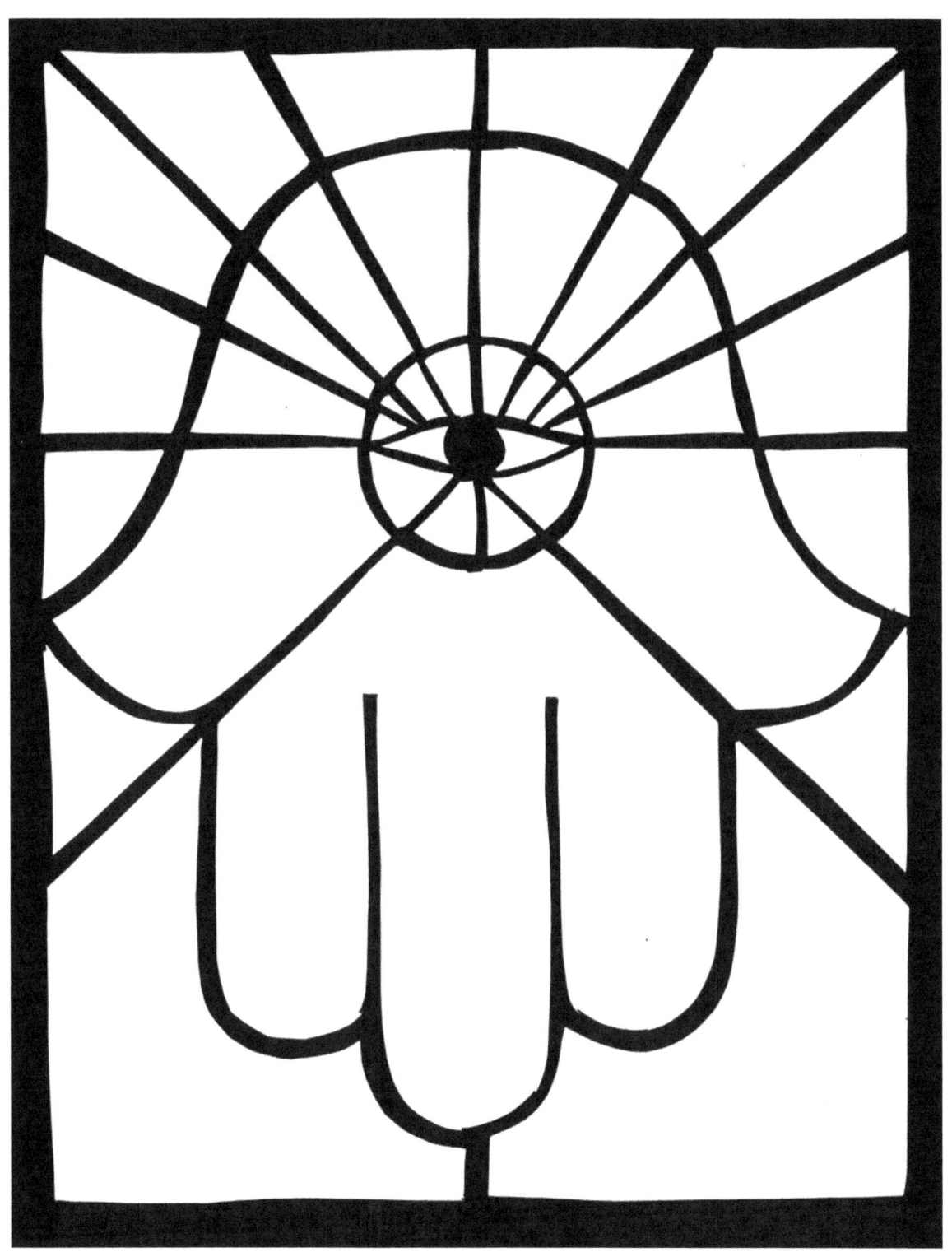

Pinchas *Numbers 25:10–30:1*

Moses describes how the land will be divided up to each tribe through a lottery. This story is represented by a *hamsa*, an ancient symbol seen in amulets used for luck and strength.

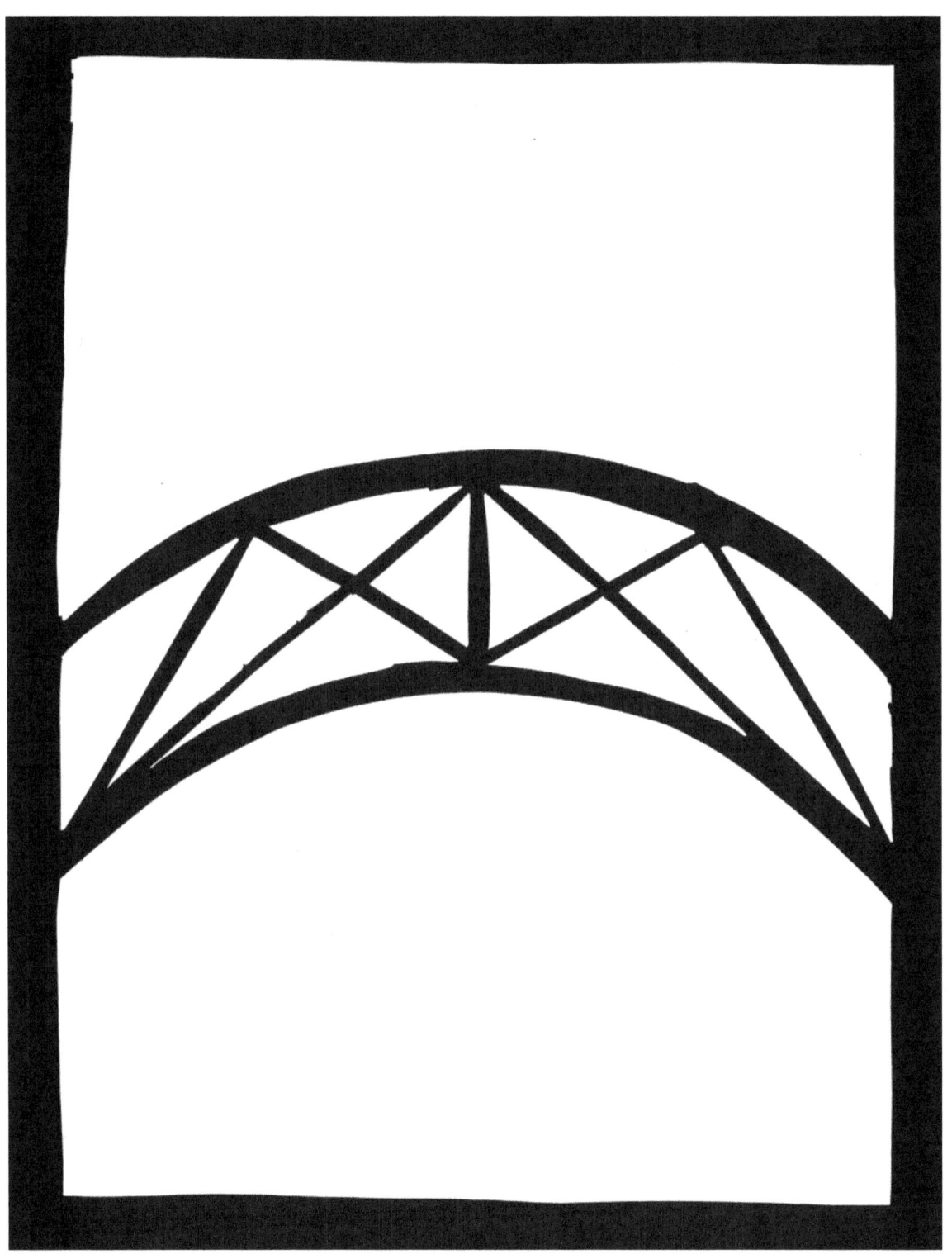

Matot *Numbers 30:2–32:42*

This story explores the tribal conflict of remaining loyal to the group vs. protecting tribal assets. The bridge highlights the conflict of the tribes of Reuben and Gad debating if they should cross over the Jordan River to conquer the land and help the other tribes, or focus on themselves.

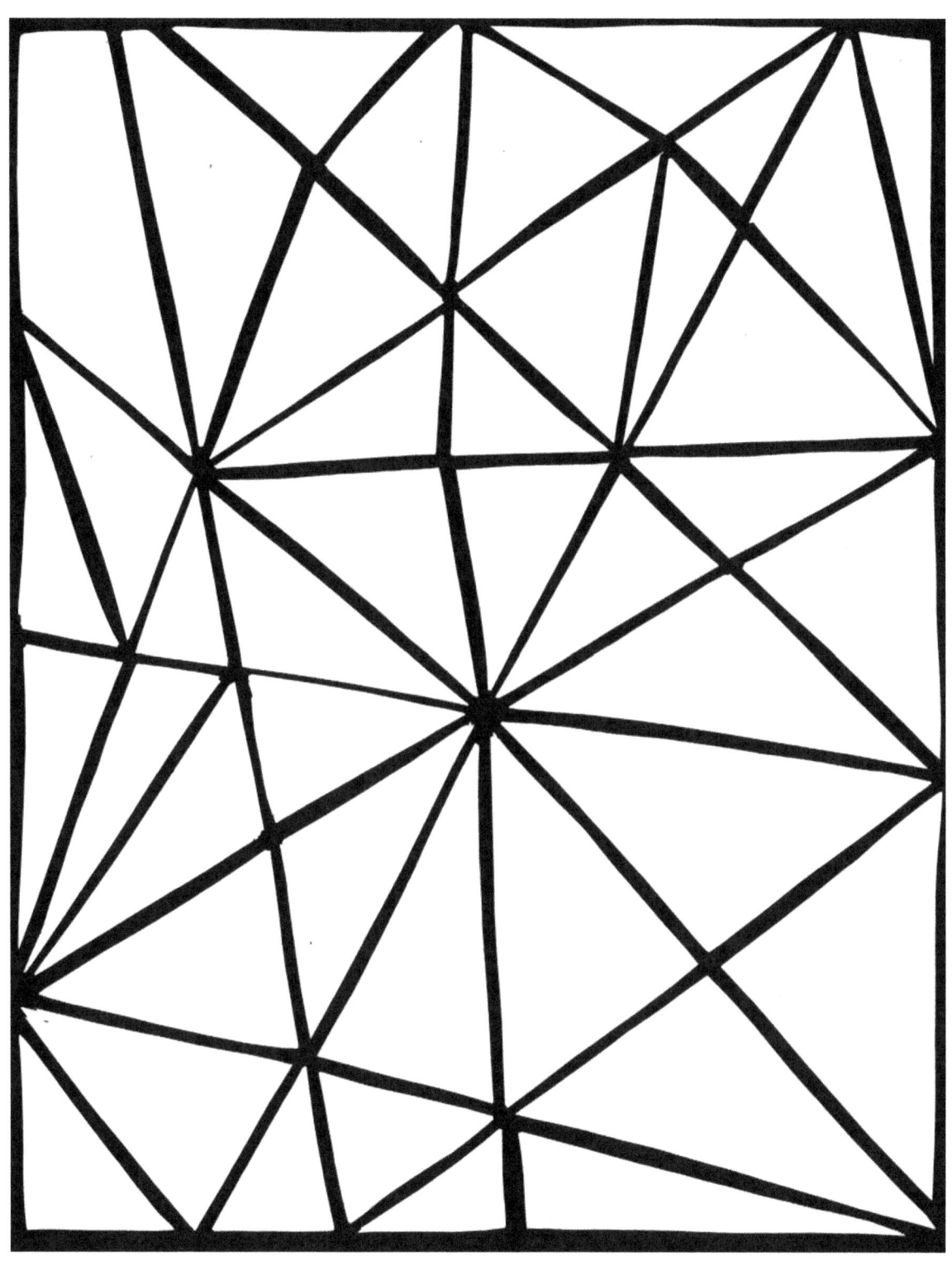

Massei *Numbers 33:1–36:13*

Moses recounts the journey of the Israelites on their travels through the desert. Their forty-two encampments over a forty year period are commemorated through forty-two triangles in this image.

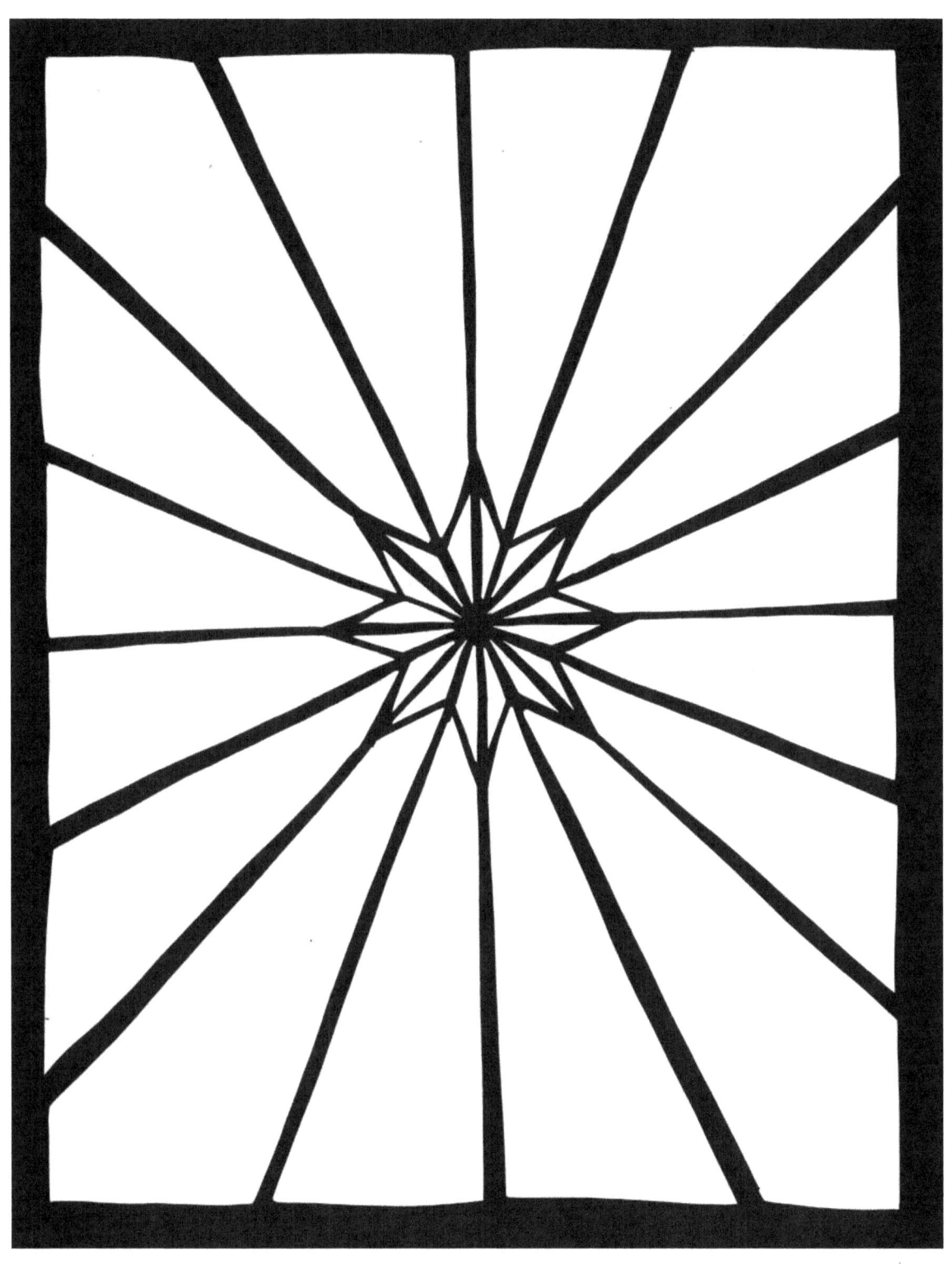

Devarim *Deuteronomy 1:1–3:22*

As he recounts the Torah, Moses repeats the promise given to Abraham, "You will be as numerous as stars in the sky," and highlights the Israelites journey from slavery to freedom.

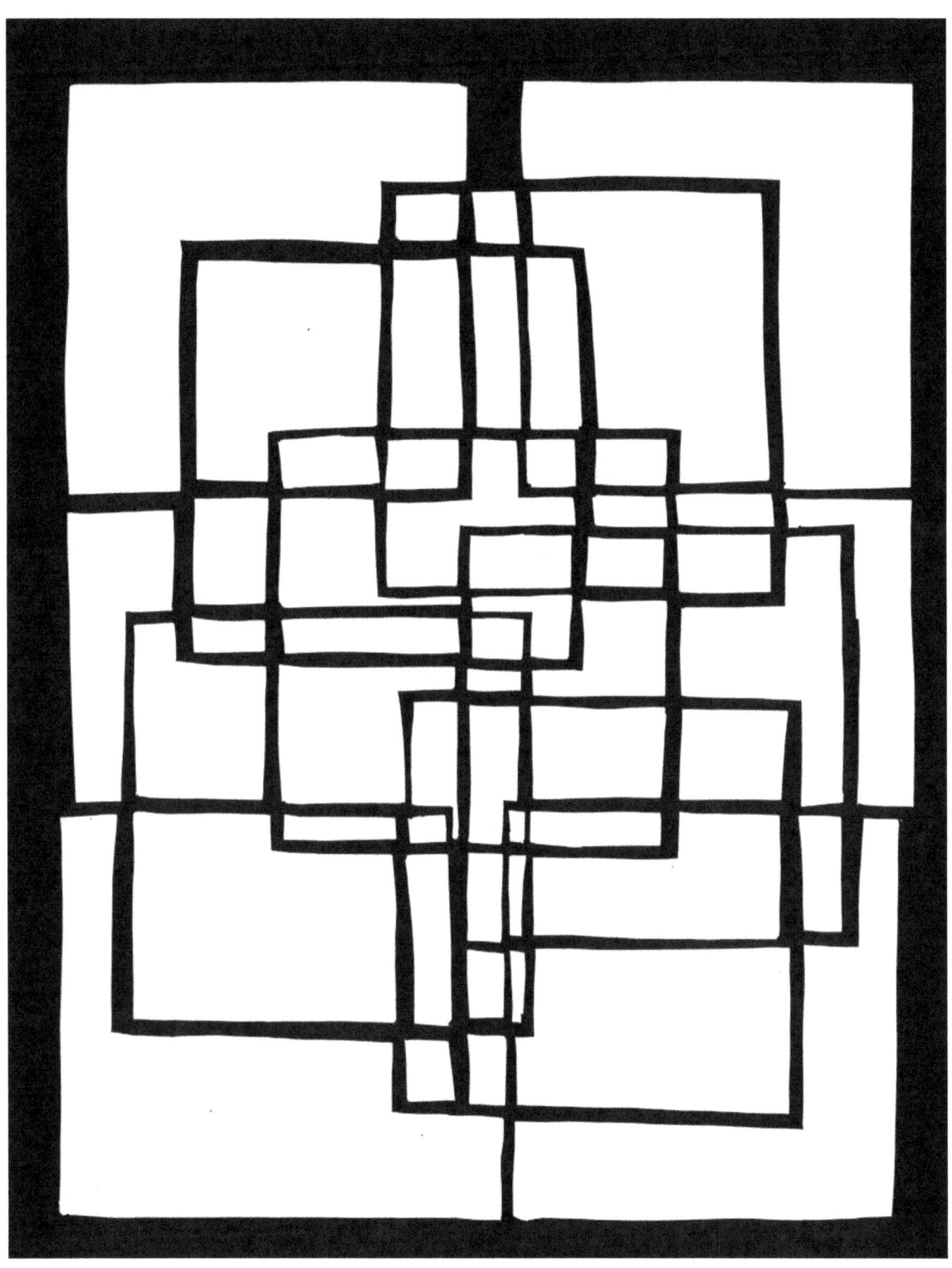

Va'etchanan *Deuteronomy 3:23–7:11*

Moses repeats the Ten Commandments in his speech to the Israelites. Depicted in this imagery are squares on top of one another to represent the boundaries and freedom of living within a set of rules.

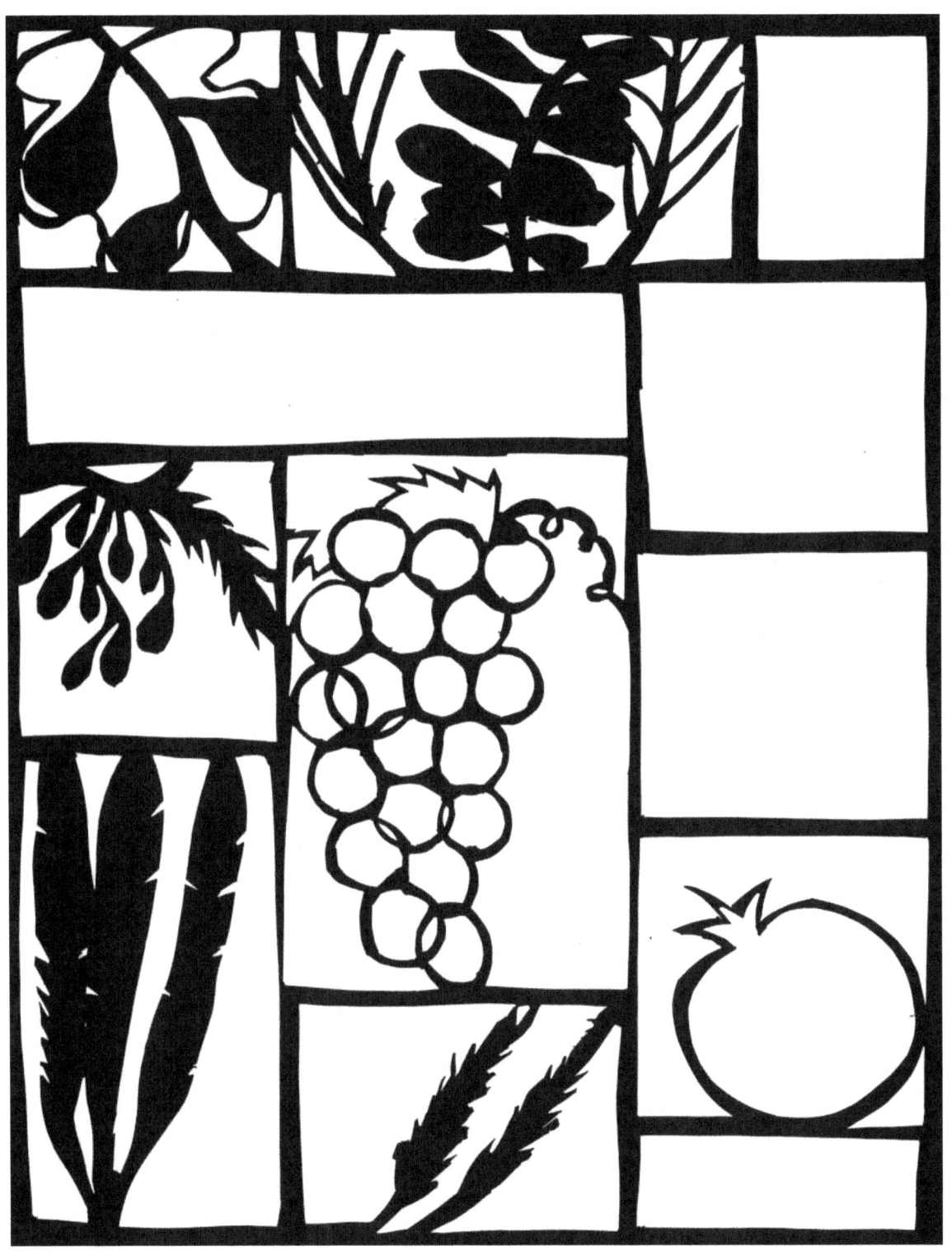

Eikev *Deuteronomy 7:12–11:25*

Moses describes the breadth of ecosystems that will be found in the Promised Land, and identifies seven different species relating to parts of the land.

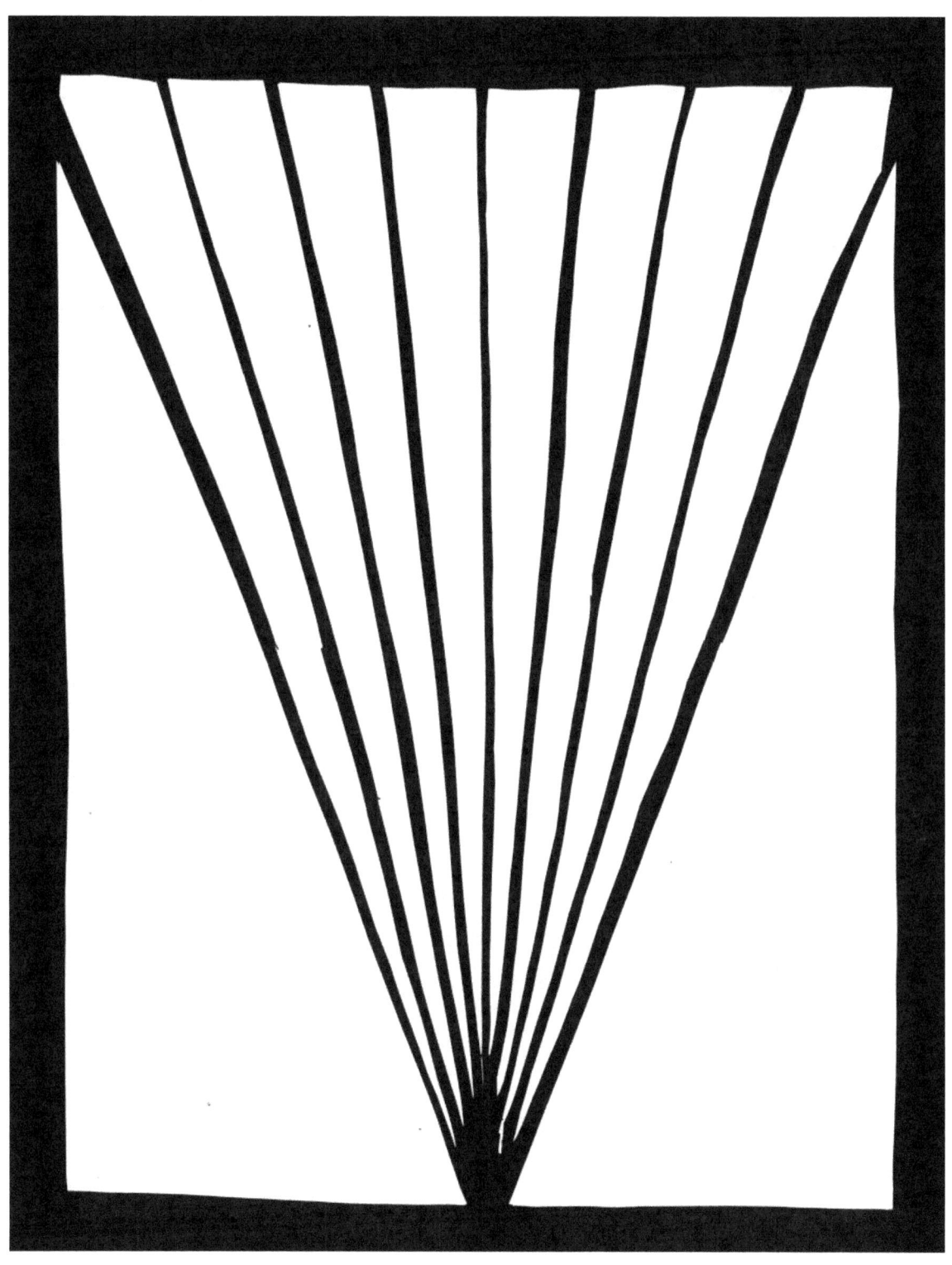

Re'eh *Deuteronomy 11:26–16:17*

Behold, I set before you today a blessing and a curse... And it will be, when the Lord, your God, will bring you to the land to which you come, to possess it, that you shall place those blessing upon Mount Gerizim, and those cursing upon Mount Ebal.

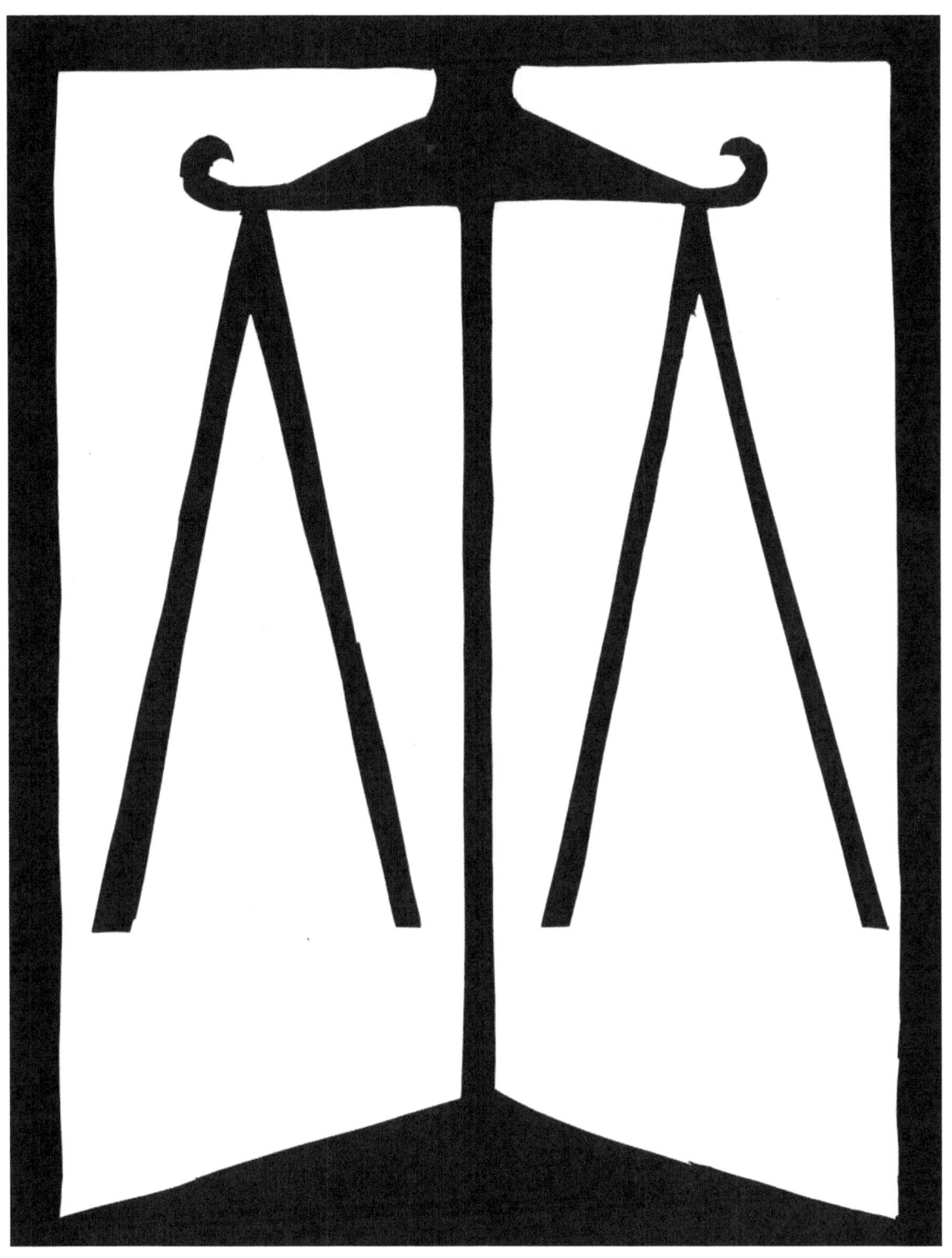

Shoftim *Deuteronomy 16:18–21:9*

Justice, Justice you shall pursue. Moses instructs the Israelites to create a system of justice by appointing judges. The empty scales reflect the level of *lightness* of a system of justice, following the harsh ways of their previous 400 years in Egypt.

Ki Teitzei *Deuteronomy 21:10–25:19*
This story instructs people to send a mother bird away before taking its eggs. While seemingly inconsequential, it serves as one of the most important commandments in the Torah.

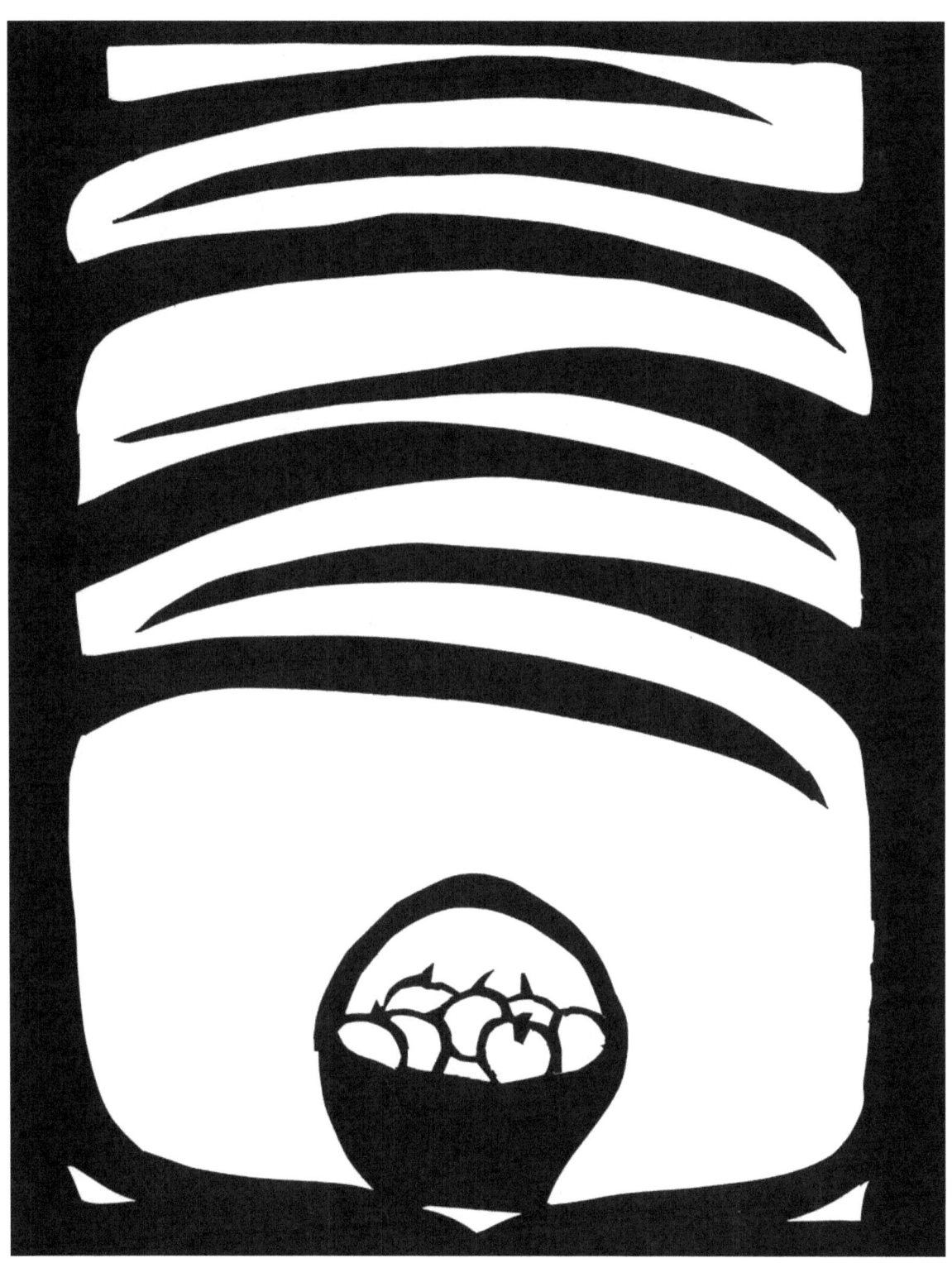

Ki Tavo *Deuteronomy 26:1-29:8*

Tithing, or offering one's first fruits to God, is instructed as a commandment for people who will transition into an agricultural life.

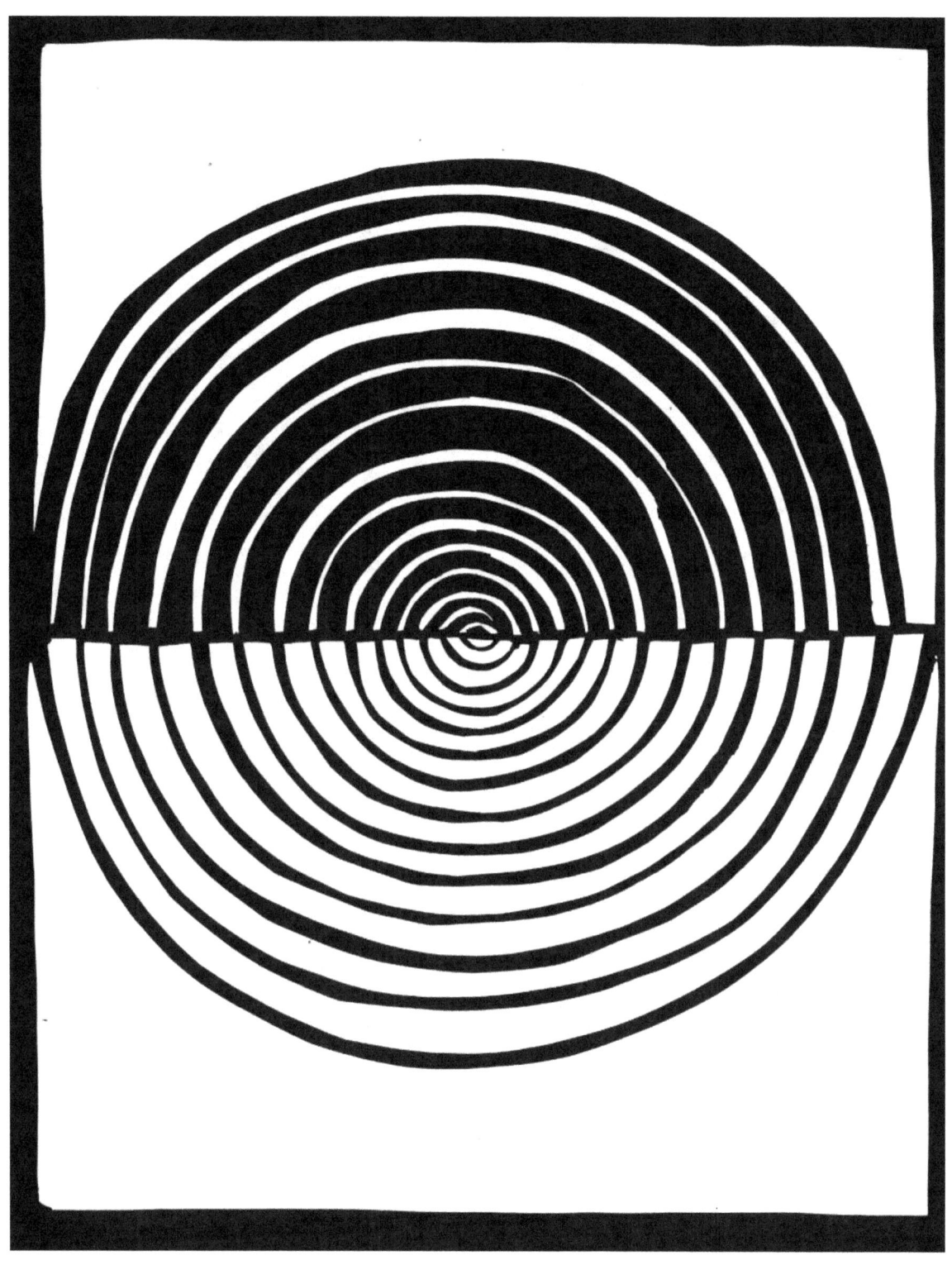

Nitzavim *Deuteronomy 29:9-30:20*

Given the opportunity for free will, the newly freed Israelites are encouraged to *choose life*. The commandment states, "I have set before you life and goodness, and death and evil: in that I command you this day to love God, to walk in His ways and to keep His commandments. Life and death I have set before you, blessing and curse. And you shall choose <u>life</u>."

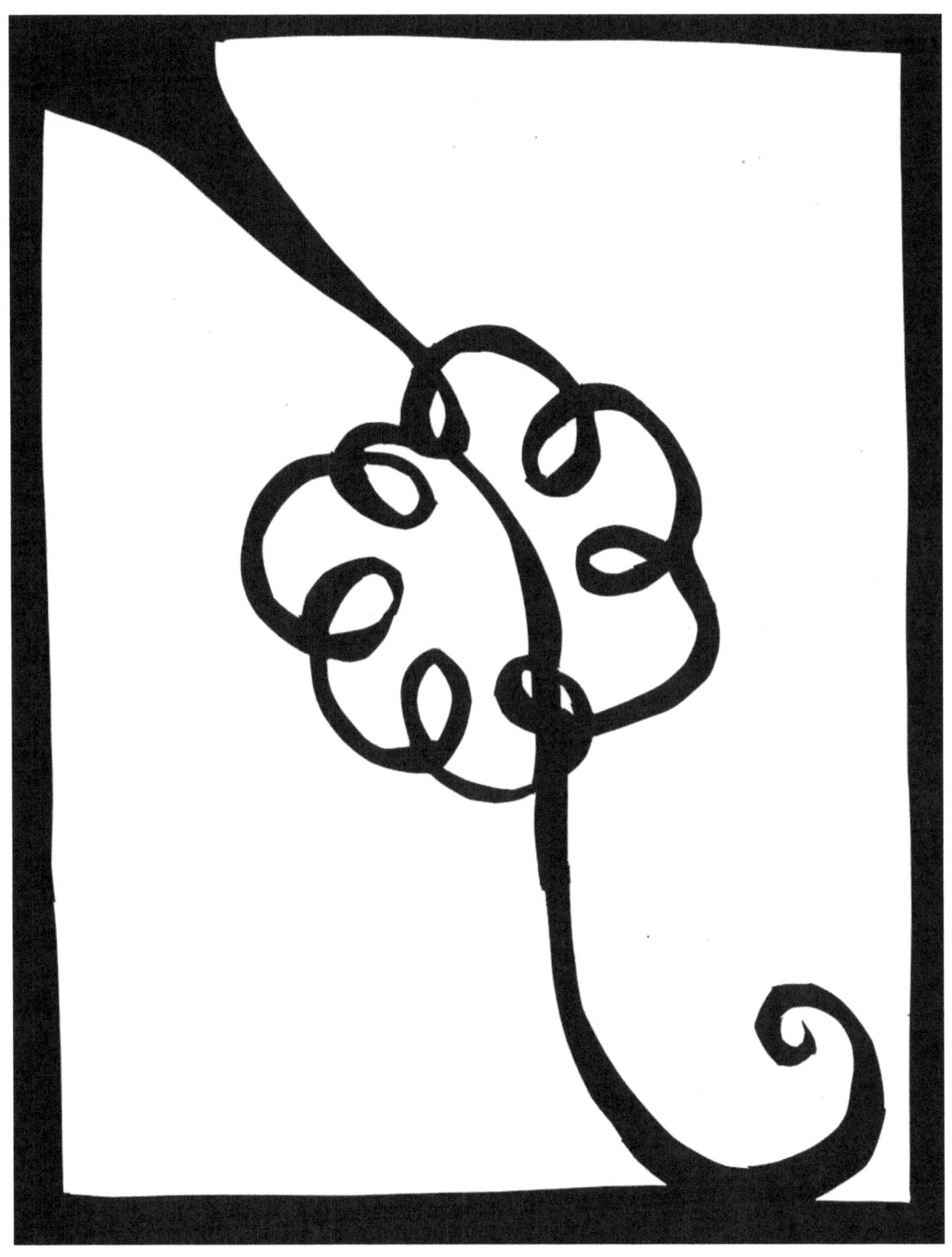

Vayelech *Deuteronomy 31:1-30*
Moses introduces the commandment of gathering, with the ritual of the entire nation convening
every seven years during the festival of Sukkot, and in the city of Jerusalem.

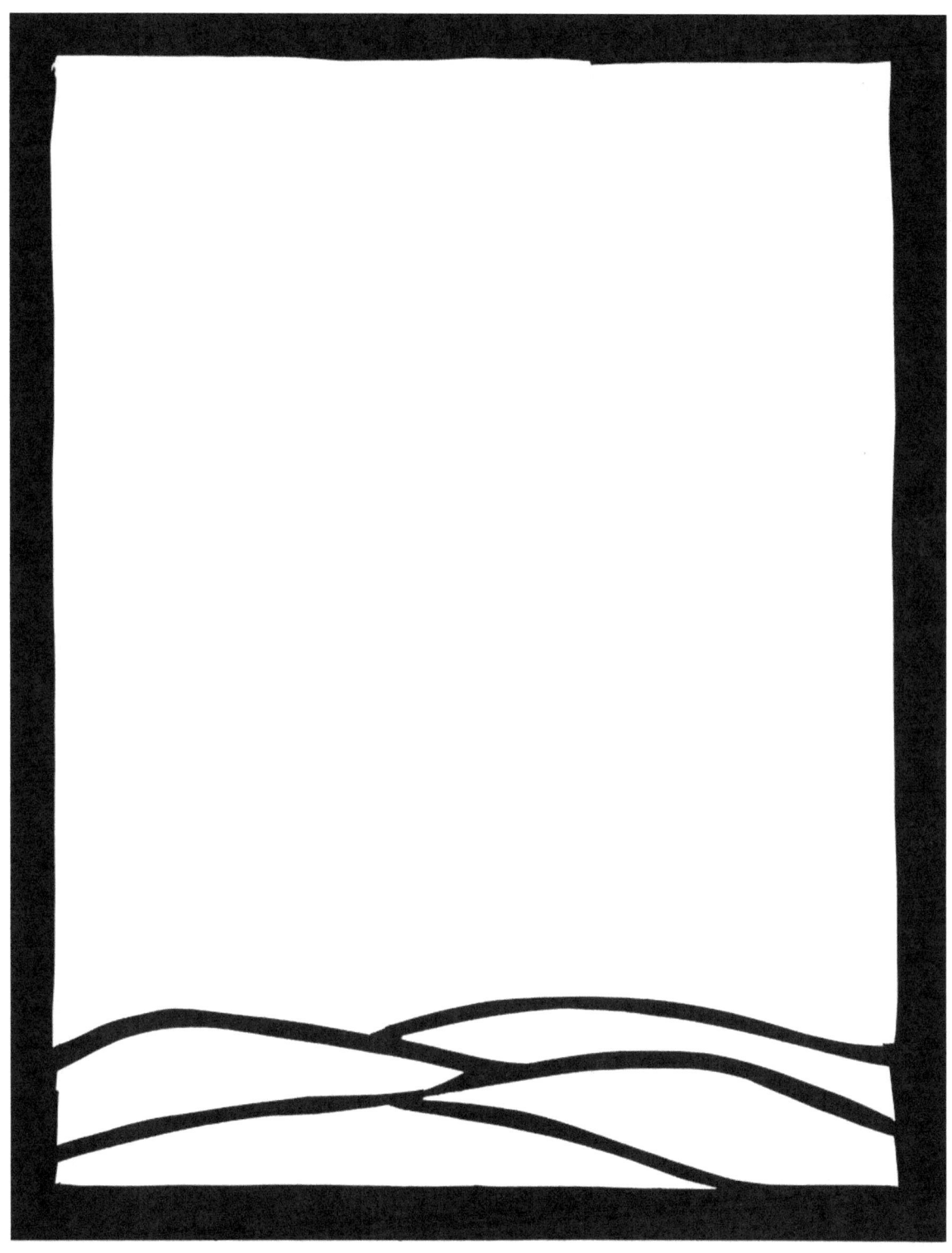

Haʾazinu *Deuteronomy 32:1-52*

Listen, O heavens, and I will speak! Let the earth hear the words of my mouth! My lesson will drip like rain; my word will flow like dew; like storm winds on vegetation and like raindrops on grass. Moses sings his final words to the tribes before the Israelites enter the Promised Land. The large sky and empty land reflect their potential, and hint at summoning the land and sky to bear witness to his words.

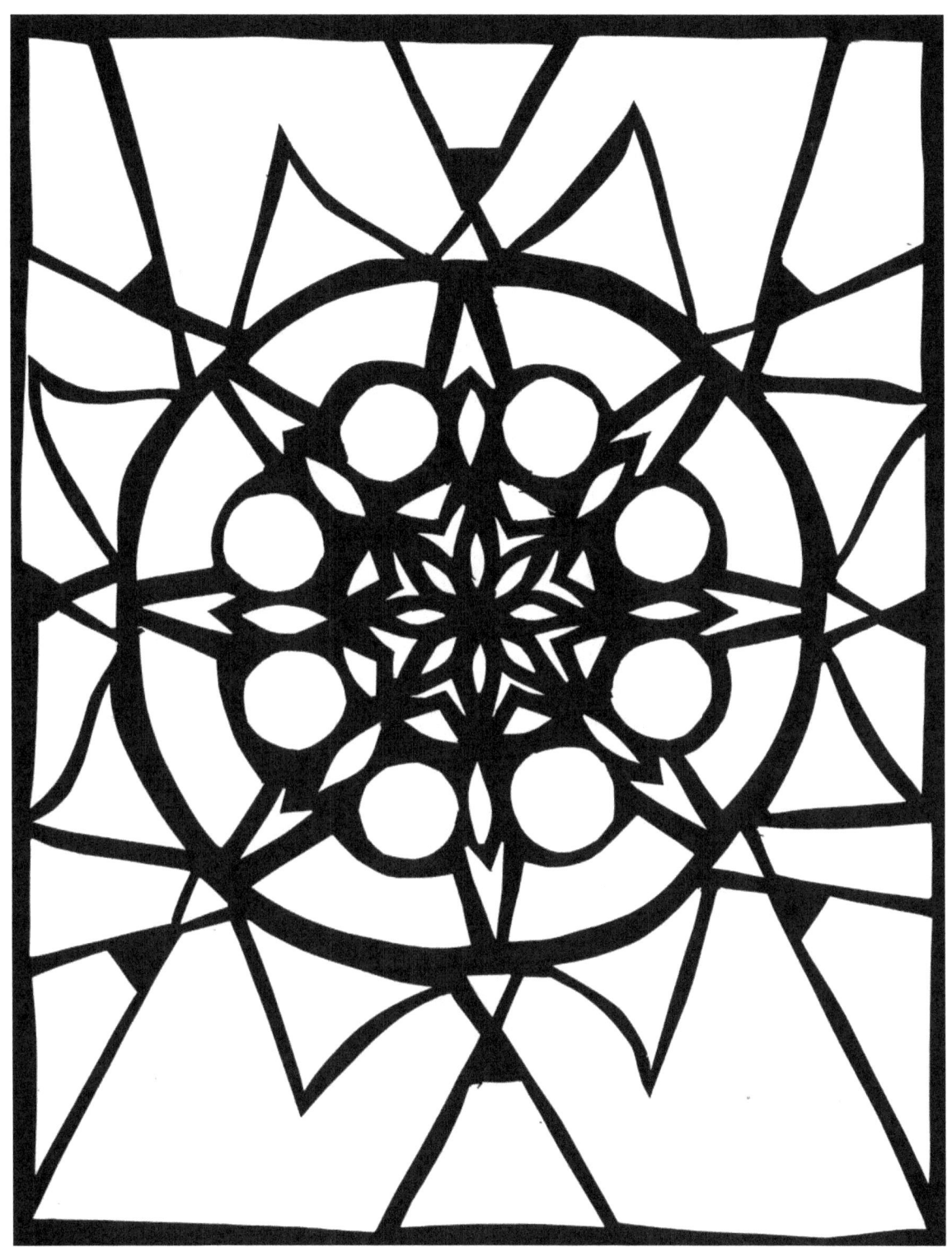

V'Zot HaBerachah *Deuteronomy 33:1-34:12*

The Israelites leave Moses behind at Mount Nebo as they enter the land of Israel. Their forty year journey in the desert comes to an end as they cross into the land. Much of this story relates to *time*, and the order of rituals throughout the year. The eight circles in the shape of a clock reflect the complex nature of a people bound by time, yet beyond time and space in their longevity as a people. The mystical significance of eight represents that which is beyond the natural order of things.

www.ingramcontent.com/pod-product-compliance
Lightning Source LLC
Chambersburg PA
CBHW060009210526
45170CB00017B/2121